MASS COMMUNICATION LAW IN PENNSYLVANIA

By Douglas S. Campbell,
Kathleen K. Olson
& Robert D. Richards

NEW
FORUMS
Stillwater, Oklahoma
U.S.A.

Table of Contents

The Authors

Douglas S. Campbell, a nationally certified paralegal, is a Professor of Journalism and Mass Communication and chair of the Department of Communication and Philosophy at Lock Haven University of Pennsylvania. He has written two books: *The Supreme Court and the Mass Media*, and *Free Press v. Fair Trial*. He earned a B.S. at the University of Maryland, an M.A. in journalism at the Pennsylvania State University, an A.M. in American Civilization at Brown University, and a doctorate in religion journalism from the Southern Methodist University.

Dr. Kathleen K. Olson is an attorney and assistant professor in the Department of Journalism and Communication at Lehigh University in Bethlehem, Pennsylvania, where she teaches media law and online journalism. She is a graduate of Northwestern University, the University of Virginia School of Law and the doctoral program in mass communication at the University of North Carolina at Chapel Hill.

Robert D. Richards is an attorney, a Professor of Journalism and Law at the Pennsylvania State University, and the founding co-director of the Pennsylvania Center for the First Amendment. The author of numerous articles on the First Amendment and of two books, *Freedom's Voice: The Perilous Present and Uncertain Future of the First Amendment* and *Uninhibited, Robust, and Wide-Open: Mr. Justice Brennan's Legacy to the First Amendment*, Richards was the winner of the PSU Dean's Award for Excellence in Research, the Dean's Award for Excellence in Service, and the Communications Alumni Society's Excellence in Teaching Award. He holds bachelors and masters degrees in speech communication from Penn State University and a doctor of jurisprudence degree from

American University and serves as associate dean for undergraduate education and director of the PSU Washington Program.

Foreword

Although not the first of its kind, this book in its second edition represents the most comprehensive and extensive study of mass communication law in Pennsylvania. The contents focus primarily on all of the most important aspects of mass communication law.

The book is designed for use by a variety of readers. Among those who would find it most helpful are students in university mass communication law courses, student reporters and editors of university and high school newspapers and year books, college and secondary school administrators, and professional reporters and editors for newspapers in Pennsylvania. Attorneys with a practice or interest in Pennsylvania mass communication law also would find this book an enlightening introduction and a beneficial overview.

Chapters have been written by authors who have demonstrated expertise in a particular subject area; and, I wish to thank Kathleen K. Olson and Robert D. Richards for their contributions to this work.

Readers should be advised that Pennsylvania statutes and cases contain a rich and extremely significant source of information about mass communication. Several landmark U.S. Supreme Court decisions in libel, for example, have origins in Pennsylvania trial and appellate courts. Moreover, Pennsylvania statutes usually reflect model federal laws and codes, resulting in Pennsylvania mass media law resting firmly in the mainstream of national laws. Thus the content of mass communication law in Pennsylvania has consequence for citizens of all states from Minnesota to New Mexico and from Virginia to California.

Douglas S. Campbell
July 2003

Chapter 1

Free Press and Fair Trial Issues

By Kathleen K. Olson

Introduction

"Publicity is the soul of justice," legal philosopher Jeremy Bentham wrote in 1827. "Without publicity, all other checks are insufficient: in comparison of publicity, all other checks are of small account."[1] Public trials enjoy a long tradition in American history, dating back to the English common law, and secret trials seem antithetical to democratic principles of openness. At the same time, the right of access to the courtroom and to court-related documents is not absolute. The First Amendment rights of the public and the press must be balanced against other rights, including the Sixth Amendment right of a criminal defendant to a trial by an "impartial jury."[2] The conflict between these rights is a serious one, and trial judges have a responsibility to protect a criminal defendant from prejudicial publicity while protecting the right of the press and the public to attend the trial and speak or write about it.

Because of the important constitutional rights at stake, the United States Supreme Court has handed down a number of

---

[1] 1 Bentham, RATIONALE OF JUDICIAL EVIDENCE 524 (1827), quoted in *Richmond Newspapers Inc. v. Virginia*, 448 U.S. 555, 569 (1980).

[2] The Sixth Amendment reads, "In all criminal prosecutions, the accused shall enjoy the right to a speedy and public trial, by an impartial jury . . . ." U.S. Const. amend. VI. The right exists at both the federal and state court levels, of course, because the Bill of Rights is applicable to the states through the Fourteenth Amendment. See *Duncan v. Louisiana*, 391 U.S. 145 (1968) (Sixth Amendment is applicable to states).

decisions that give the lower courts guidelines for balancing the competing rights. In the 1966 landmark case *Sheppard v. Maxwell*, the Supreme Court set forth a list of tools for trial judges to use to combat prejudicial publicity without violating the First Amendment. Among them are the continuance, change of venue, jury sequestration, and *voir dire*, or careful jury selection to make sure the jurors can put aside any exposure to prejudicial publicity.[3]

While none of these tools is perfect, the Supreme Court has made clear that more extreme measures to limit prejudicial publicity are prohibited. Direct gag orders on the press, for example, are effective but are limited to extreme circumstances because they constitute prior restraint – that is, they prevent the speech from ever being heard. Gag orders, to be constitutional, must be justified by a compelling interest, must be narrowly tailored and must only be used when no other alternatives are available to ensure a fair trial.[4] Trial judges find it easier, therefore, to impose gag orders on trial participants than directly on the media. In July 2002, for example, a Philadelphia municipal court judge imposed a gag order on the police, the district attorney's office and defense lawyers to keep them from discussing criminal charges filed against basketball star Allen Iverson.[5]

Another extreme measure to combat prejudicial publicity is closing the courtroom to the press and public. In 1980, however, the U.S. Supreme Court ruled that closing the courtroom to the press is unconstitutional, at least in some circumstances. In *Richmond Newspapers, Inc. v. Virginia*, the Court held that the First Amendment requires that criminal trials be open to the public absent an overriding interest articulated in

---

[3] See *Sheppard v. Maxwell*, 384 U.S. 333, 357-363 (1966).
[4] *Nebraska Press Assn. v. Stuart*, 427 U.S. 539 (1976).
[5] Michael Rubinkam, *Gag Order Issued in Iverson Case*, Associated Press (July 22, 2002).

findings by the court.[6] The Court based its ruling on the long tradition of public criminal trials in the United States and England as well as the functional role that openness can play in a democratic government. Public oversight of trials helps ensure that fairness prevails, the Court said, by discouraging misbehavior on the part of parties and witnesses and abuse of power by judges and prosecutors.[7]

The Court returned to the issue of public access in subsequent cases and offered further guidance as to how courts should weigh competing concerns, although it left open how its holding in *Richmond Newspapers* should be applied to civil trials and administrative proceedings. In general, the Court's line of rulings established some basic principles regarding courtroom access. First, while the right of public access is strong, it is not absolute and must be weighed against countervailing interests, which may include the defendant's Sixth Amendment right to a fair trial. Second, in balancing these interests with regard to criminal proceedings, courts must apply a strict scrutiny standard: the interest must be compelling and the closure must be narrowly tailored to serve that interest.

Pennsylvania Court Proceedings
Criminal proceedings

While Pennsylvania courts are required to follow the U.S. Supreme Court's rulings, state common law and the Pennsylvania Constitution provide additional support for the principle of openness. Pennsylvania's state constitution not only guarantees criminal defendants "a speedy public trial," it also states plainly that "all courts shall be open."[8] Despite this plain language, the Pennsylvania Supreme Court in

---

[6] *Richmond Newspapers, Inc. v. Virginia*, 448 U.S. 555, 581 (1980).

[7] *Richmond Newspapers, Inc.*, 569.

[8] Pa. Const. art. I, 9 ("In all criminal prosecutions the accused hath a right to ... a speedy and public trial by an impartial jury of the vicinage."); Pa. Const. art. I, 11.

Commonwealth v. Hayes denied that it means what it says: "[O]ur research of the appellate decisional law fails to uncover any support for the claim that [the] open court provision provides a greater right of access to the public in criminal trials than the public trial provisions of the federal and state Constitutions."[9] Thus, the Court in *Hayes* ruled that the right of public access is not absolute and must yield to the defendant's right to a fair trial.

Still, closure of the courtroom should not be ordered "where there is an effective and efficient alternative means to assure the accused's fair trial rights."[10] The Court ruled that the trial court's closure of a pretrial suppression hearing was not constitutional because sequestration of the jury was a reasonable alternative to closing the hearing and would not jeopardize the defendant's right to a fair trial.

In 1982, the Court of Appeals for the Third Circuit (the federal appeals court governing Pennsylvania) found in *United States v. Criden* that "the same societal interests and structural arguments that mandated a First Amendment right of access to criminal trials" in *Richmond Newspapers* applied with equal force to pretrial criminal proceedings. The court therefore ruled that the public had a First Amendment right of access to pretrial suppression hearings.[11] The Pennsylvania Supreme Court in *Commonwealth v. Buehl* agreed with the Third Circuit's reasoning and adopted its holding, saying, "If justice is to be done, and is to be seen as done, if the courts are to fulfill their proper role as one branch in our system of government, the public must have access both to the trial and to the pretrial proceedings."[12]

---

[9] *Commonwealth v. Hayes*, 414 A.2d 318, 322, *cert. denied*, 449 U.S. 992 (1980).

[10] *Commonwealth v. Hayes*, 428.

[11] *United States v. Criden*, 675 F.2d 550, 557 (3d Cir. 1982).

[12] *Commonwealth v. Buehl*, 462 A.2d 1316, 1321 (Pa.Super. 1983).

The Court in *Buehl* also echoed the Third Circuit's *Criden* decision by setting up specific procedures for Pennsylvania trial judges to follow when considering courtroom closure. In *Criden*, the Third Circuit ruled that motions for closure of suppression hearings must be posted on the court docket and that the trial court must consider alternatives to closure and must state on the record the reasons for rejecting those alternatives in order to allow for appellate review of the decision.[13] Similarly, the *Buehl* court required that trial judges give ample notice to the public that a motion to close the proceeding is before the court and provide an opportunity for the public to be heard on the matter. The court must also articulate on the record its consideration of the available alternatives to closure and must state *before* ordering closure why it considers those alternatives unsatisfactory.[14]

In all cases, the presumption of public access is rebuttable and the rights of the criminal defendant under the Sixth Amendment must be protected. Still, the right of public access is a strong one, and the trial court must have good reasons to close the courtroom. Along with pretrial suppression hearings, the Third Circuit and the Pennsylvania Supreme Court have ruled that the right of public access extends to post-trial hearings to investigate possible juror misconduct,[15] to the testimony of a key witness during a criminal trial,[16] and to jury selection.[17]

Civil proceedings

Pennsylvania courts follow two lines of analysis with regard to public access to civil proceedings, one based on the First Amendment and one based in common law. Although the

---

[13] *United States v. Criden*, 554.
[14] *Commonwealth v. Buehl*, 1323.
[15] *United States v. Simone*, 14 F.3d 833 (3d Cir. 1994).
[16] *Commonwealth v. Contakos*, 453 A.2d 578 (Pa. 1982).
[17] *Commonwealth v. Johnson*, 455 A.2d 654 (Pa.Super. 1982).

U.S. Supreme Court has yet to rule on whether the First Amendment extends the right of public access to civil trials, in Pennsylvania that issue has been settled. In 1984, the Third Circuit asked, "Does the First Amendment secure to the public and to the press a right of access to civil proceedings?" and answered yes.[18] In *Publicker Industries, Inc. v. Cohen*, the court found a right of access to civil trials based both in history and in the Supreme Court's *Richmond Newspapers* First Amendment analysis.

The court found that a tradition of access has long existed with regard to civil trials as well as criminal trials and that the beneficial effects of public access were the same: "Public access to civil trials, no less than criminal trials, plays an important role in the participation and the free discussion of governmental affairs." [19] Therefore, the court held, the First Amendment protects a right of access to civil trials in order to ensure that this discussion is an informed one.

In order to limit public access, the court said, there must be a showing that limiting access "serves an important governmental interest" and that there is no less restrictive way to serve that interest.[20] The party seeking closure bears the burden of showing that the material is the kind of information that courts will protect and that there is "good cause" for closure, meaning that denial will "work a clearly defined and serious injury" to the party seeking closure.[21] As in criminal proceedings, the court must articulate the countervailing interest it seeks to protect and make specific findings so that a reviewing court can determine whether the closure order was proper.[22]

---

[18] *Publicker Industries, Inc. v. Cohen*, 733 F.2d 1059, 1061 (3d Cir. 1984).
[19] *Publicker Industries, Inc.*, 1070.
[20] *Publicker Industries, Inc.*, 1070.
[21] *Publicker Industries, Inc.*, 1071.
[22] *Publicker Industries, Inc.*, 1070-1071.

Pennsylvania state courts have followed *Publicker* and have found a strong presumption of openness for civil proceedings, based on both the First Amendment and the Pennsylvania Constitution. In order for a proceeding to be closed, the moving party must show that the "material is the kind of information that the courts will protect and that there is good cause for the order to issue."[23]

The standard for civil proceedings is lower than that for criminal trials – the interest favoring closure can be "important" rather than "compelling" – so the presumption of openness is easier to overcome. Indeed, the Pennsylvania Rules of Civil Procedure grant discretion to a trial court to exclude the public from civil proceedings in the interest of "public good, order or morals."[24]

Interests that may constitute good cause for closure vary and may go to the content of the information at issue, the relationship of the parties, or the nature of the controversy itself. The need to protect a trade secret, for example, may overcome the presumption of openness and warrant closure. State law bars the public from certain juvenile proceedings in order to protect the privacy of minors, although the court has discretion to allow access.[25] In *Katz v. Katz*, the Pennsylvania Superior Court ruled that divorce hearings were the type of proceeding that could be closed at the discretion of the court. Although the court did not rule specifically on what might constitute "good

---

[23] *Hutchison v. Luddy,* 581 A.2d 578, 582 (Pa.Super. 1990).

[24] Pa.R.Civ.P. 223. The rule states that, subject to the requirements of due process and the constitutional rights of the parties, the court may make and enforce rules:

> (4) Regulating or excluding the public or persons not interested in the proceedings whenever the court deems such regulation or exclusion to be in the interest of the public good, order or morals.

[25] 42 *Pa.C.S.A.* 6336(d).

cause" in that case, it suggested that the right to keep certain financial and family matters private might warrant closure.[26]

The second line of public access analysis in Pennsylvania is based on a common law approach that emphasizes a balancing of interests. Under this method, the party seeking closure must show that "the interest in secrecy outweighs the presumption" of openness.[27] In *R.W. v. Hampe*, the Pennsylvania Superior Court applied the common law balancing test to rule that the plaintiff in a medical malpractice case could not hide her identity by using only her initials in the court records. Because the suit involved psychiatric care, the plaintiff claimed that revealing her identity would cause her "extreme, unnecessary embarrassment" and that this interest outweighed the presumption of openness.[28] The court recognized the policy behind limiting identification in cases involving minors or "incompetents," but found that policy was inapplicable here. "[T]his is not a private matter such as a divorce or a mental health proceeding," the court said, "but rather an adversarial proceeding which has a 'public purpose.'"[29] Thus even under the common law balancing test, the plaintiff had not shown that her interest in secrecy outweighed the general presumption of openness.

Court documents

The right of public access to trials includes the right to inspect the documentation of the proceedings, so court pleadings[30] and hearing transcripts[31] are presumptively open to

---

[26] *Katz v. Katz*, 514 A.2d 1374 (Pa.Super. 1986).

[27] *Bank of America Nat'l Trust & Savings Ass'n v. Hotel Rittenhouse Ass'n,* 800 F.2d 339, 344 (3d Cir.1986).

[28] *R.W. v. Hampe,* 626 A.2d 1218, 1219 (Pa.Super. 1993).

[29] *R.W. v. Hampe,* 1223, citing *Katz v. Katz,* 514 A.2d 1374 (Pa.Super. 1986).

[30] *Nixon v. Warner Communications, Inc.*, 435 U.S. 589 (1978); *Stenger v. Lehigh Valley Hospital Center*, 554 A.2d 954, 960 (Pa.Super. 1989).

[31] *United States v. Antar*, 38 F.3d 1348 (3d Cir. 1994).

the public in Pennsylvania in both civil and criminal proceedings. In general, any document that is filed with a court is considered a "judicial record" and is therefore subject to public disclosure. The Pennsylvania Superior Court has also recognized a First Amendment-based right of access to such documents as probable cause affidavits[32] and search warrants.[33]

The presumption of openness does not extend to discovery documents, however, because they are generally not filed with the court.[34]   Thus in *Stenger v. Lehigh Valley Hospital Center*, the Pennsylvania Superior Court ruled that *The Morning Call* of Allentown had no right of access to discovery materials that included information about the plaintiffs' "sexual practices, their idiosyncrasies, and their personal hygiene habits."[35] The court ruled that the court's protective order was a proper exercise of its discretion under the Pennsylvania Rules of Civil Procedure[36] and was not a violation of *The Morning Call*'s First Amendment rights or common law rights of access to judicial records.

Finally, because of the state interest in protecting the privacy of minors, state law limits access to court records in juvenile proceedings to parties "having a legitimate interest" in the proceedings.[37]   Media interest is not generally considered sufficient to constitute a "legitimate interest" in these cases.

Administrative hearings

Administrative hearings are civil proceedings but they involve "fundamentally different procedures" and lack the "long

---

[32] *Commonwealth v. Fenstermaker*, 530 A.2d 414, 418 (Pa. 1987).

[33] *PG Publishing Co. v. Commonwealth,* 614 A.2d 1106 (Pa. 1992).

[34] *Seattle Times Co. v. Rhinehart*, 467 U.S. 20 (1984); *Kurtzman v. Hankin*, 714 A.2d 450 (Pa.Super. 1998).

[35] *Stenger v. Lehigh Valley Hospital Center*, 959.

[36] The rules allow a court, in its discretion, to implement a protective order sealing discovery materials or a deposition to save a party from "unreasonable embarrassment, annoyance or burden." Pa.R.Civ.P. 4012.

[37] 42 *Pa.C.S.A.* 6307.

history of openness" upon which public access to criminal and civil trials has been based.[38] Thus the Third Circuit ruled in 1986 that the state's interests in preserving limited confidentiality in judicial disciplinary proceedings outweighed any presumption of openness that may attach to such proceedings.[39]

Similarly, the Third Circuit ruled in 2002 that, despite Immigration and Naturalization Service regulations making deportation proceedings presumptively open to the public, cases "of special interest" – that is, those involving individuals suspected of having ties to terrorism – could be completely closed to the public and press after the terrorist attacks of September 11, 2001. The Third Circuit held that there is no First Amendment right to attend deportation proceedings.[40] In a similar case, however, the Sixth Circuit ruled that the First Amendment *did* create a right of access to such proceedings.[41] The U.S. Supreme Court refused to hear the Third Circuit case on appeal[42] but may agree to hear the Sixth Circuit case in order to resolve the conflict between the circuit courts. The legal fight to open deportation proceedings may therefore give the Supreme Court an opportunity to revisit the important issue of public access and resolve lingering questions about the reach of its holding in *Richmond Newspapers*.

Cameras in the courtroom

In 1980, the U.S. Supreme Court ruled that the presence of television cameras is not inherently prejudicial, but left room for individual criminal defendants to argue that the presence of

---

[38] *First Amendment Coalition v. Judicial Inquiry & Review Bd.*, 784 F.2d 467, 472 (3d Cir. 1986).

[39] *First Amendment Coalition*, 472.

[40] *North Jersey Media Group v. Ashcroft*, 308 F.3d 198 (3d Cir. 2002).

[41] *Detroit Free Press v. Ashcroft*, 303 F.3d 681 (6th Cir. 2002).

[42] *North Jersey Media Group v. Ashcroft*, 155 L.Ed. 2d 1106, 2003 U.S. LEXIS 4082, 71 U.S.L.W. 3734 (2003) (denying certiorari).

cameras during their own trials had violated their rights.[43] Today, television cameras and still photography remain relatively rare in Pennsylvania courtrooms, Court TV notwithstanding. Rule 112 of the Pennsylvania Rules of Criminal Procedure requires Pennsylvania courts to prohibit "the taking of photographs, video, or motion pictures of any judicial proceedings or in the hearing room or courtroom or its environs during the judicial proceedings."[44] The Pennsylvania Superior Court held in 1993 that the courtroom's "environs" included the front lawn of a crime scene where a jury viewing took place and that the judge had the authority to ban photography there and to confiscate a television station's videotape.[45]

In civil proceedings, the judge may allow the use of courtroom cameras in non-jury cases, as long as all parties agree and the use of cameras will not "distort or dramatize the proceeding."[46] Support, custody or divorce proceedings are exempt from this rule.

In the federal courts, electronic media coverage of criminal cases has been expressly prohibited under Federal Rule of Criminal Procedure 53 since the criminal rules were adopted in 1946. In 1972, the Judicial Conference of the United States adopted a prohibition against "broadcasting, televising, recording, or taking photographs in the courtroom and areas immediately adjacent thereto... ." The prohibition, which was contained in the Code of Conduct for United States Judges, applied to both criminal and civil cases.

Although the U.S. District Court for the Eastern District of Pennsylvania participated in a three-year pilot program experimenting with cameras in the courtroom in the early

---

[43] *Chandler v. Florida*, 449 U.S. 560 (1981).

[44] Pa.R.Crim.P. 112(A)(1).

[45] *Commonwealth v. Davis*, 635 A.2d 1062 (Pa.Super. 1993) (interpreting former Rule 328).

[46] Pa. Supreme Court Code of Judicial Conduct Canon 3A(7)(d).

1990s, cameras are no longer allowed in federal trials there. In addition, cameras are not allowed in the appellate courts in Pennsylvania, either at the state or federal level.

Chapter 2

Pennsylvania Libel Law

by Douglas S. Campbell

One of the earliest recorded objections to speaking libelous words can be found in the Mosaic code: Exodus 22:28, "Do not blaspheme God or curse the ruler of your people." Roman--and later British and American law--continued this notion of what is known today as seditious libel, that is, libel of the government (*famosus libellus*). It is based on the assumption that speech defaming the government or its leaders in essence constitutes treason because it could result in the overthrow of governmental leaders or even of the government itself. Consequently, sever punishments were inflicted on persons convicted of seditious libel. The Romans did not hesitate to use execution and the British resorted to hanging, drawing and quartering, cropping ears, slitting noses, imprisonment, and the pillory.

One aspect of seditious libel was applied in both Britain and America to private citizens: the belief that defamation could be calculated purposely to cause a breach of the peace. The most common expression of such a breach is dueling. Laws, therefore, were passed against it, making criminal this form of libel. In prosecuting such libel, jurists asserted that the greater the truth, the greater the libel because it was thought that truth was more likely to stir someone to illegal action, such as a duel, than was falsehood.

Parallel to this idea of criminal libel was the concept of civil libel. The damage caused by civil libel is not breach of peace, but injury to reputation. Thus, in civil libel concern for personal character replaces concern for public order. Interestingly enough, the ascension of civil libel corresponds roughly with the advent of newspapers. Slander was the main concern of governments before the printing press was invented simply because written works then were usually devoted to religious topics and so rarely libelous. Slander often became associated with seditious or criminal defamation and libel with private or civil defamation. During the sixteenth century libel suits became rampant.

Although seditious libel appears at first glance to be the equivalent of verbal treason, important differences can be identified. In seventeen and eighteenth century England, for example, seditious libel was unprotected speech, not so much because it threatened immanent violent overthrow of government, but because it "scandalized government." The basic fault of seditious libel was its "bad tendency" (what Blackstone termed "a pernicious tendency"). The tendency of seditious libel, quite simply, was to elicit contempt or hatred of the government and the governors; these opprobrious attitudes, it was thought, threaten political harmony and peace and so undermine the confidence of citizens in their government and governors. The damage caused by seditious libel, therefore, was not necessarily the encouragement of an immediate illegal or treasonous action, such as a breach of peace, but the turning of citizens against their government. As a lesser crime than treason, seditious libel merited less severe--although at times what we today would consider cruel--punishment.

Seeds for late twentieth-century concepts of libel were planted in the America debates over the 1798 Sedition Act. One argument against seditious libel was that, whereas sovereignty in England rests in the government because of the notion that parliament--like the king previously--can do no wrong, in American democracy sovereignty rests not in the government itself, but in the people who elect the governors. Consequently, the people should be able to say whatever they wish about the government and their governors without fear of being charged with libel.

Indeed, some argued that even false criticism of the government is not libelous. These critics asserted that fact and opinion were often indistinguishable, that opinions were not provable as true, and that there exists a variety of truths, many of which cannot be supported by the kind of evidence required in a courtroom. To assert that a false statement about the government would result in disrespect for it, breach of peace, or even violent overthrow, these critics argued, is to assume wrongly that citizens cannot differentiate truth from error.

Another important twentieth-century concept with roots in the sedition debates is malice. Some Libertarian critics of the Act were willing to allow false criticism of the State as long as it was not made with purposeful intent to subvert the government or to bring it into hatred or contempt. This idea was based on the notion that the power to punish libel against government derived from a nation's inherent right of self-protection. Such a position raised the additional problem of distinguishing between presumed and actual malice.

One eventual result of these debates was an 1805 New York statute that, in some respects, became the model for much of the rest of the country for more than a century. It gave the jury--not the judge--power to decide whether a libel was criminal and permitted truth as a defense if it was published with good motives and for justifiable ends.

As the nineteenth century opened, the rise of a more literate society reading newspapers presented new problems. To satisfy democratic citizens hungering for news of their government and its leaders in all branches, the concept of privilege emerged. At bottom, this concept gives limited protection from libel suits for news reports based on official governmental records, meetings, or deliberations.

The defense of fair comment also was born during this same period. Courts began to assert that, in order for a democracy to function effectively, journalists should be allowed to express opinions or fair comments upon matters of public interest.

New York Times v. *Sullivan* represents a watershed in libel theory.[1] Asserting in sharp contrast to the 1798 notions of seditious libel--which were based on the assumption that self-preservation requires governors and government be protected from libel--the justices in this case said that the governors (what the court called public officials), need less, not more, protection than private citizens. Such a view reflects the ideas of Libertarian Sedition Act critics who asserted that a free press is necessary to service a democratic political system. In other words, a democracy cannot function efficiently or justly unless the voters are fully informed about governmental officials who make decisions that affect the lives of all citizens.

Borrowing the idea of "breathing space" from *NAACP* v. *Button*,[2] Brennan asserts in *Sullivan* that some error in public debate must be tolerated and protected by the Constitution if truth is to be fully liberated. To guarantee this breathing space for error, the Court invented a new definition for actual (in contrast to presumed) malice. By requiring public officials to demonstrate a high level of fault, this new concept of actual malice places a heavy burden on a public officials who seek to prove a false statement is libelous. These officials must show that an author either knew a libelous statement was false or exhibited a reckless disregard for its truth. In short, this breathing space includes false statements made in good faith because the Court felt the First Amendment requires some false ideas to be protected in order to guarantee that the full truth is heard. It said that error is inevitable in any vigorous debate and so some error must be tolerated in public debates in order to

---

[1]376 U.S. 254 (1964).
[2]371 U.S. 415 (1963).

avoid deterring attempts to express unpopular, but truthful, statements.

Since the actual malice privilege protects only criticism of public officials, this decision set off a long series of clarifications of what is a public official. One approach says that libel plaintiffs must overcome the actual malice privilege whenever circumstances giving rise to a libel case concern matters of public interest. Another says the test centers not on the public or private nature of the circumstances, but on the public or private nature of the persons defamed. For the most part--*Rosenbloom* v. *Metromedia*[3] is the notable exception-- there the Court used a combination of the two: subject matter and nature of person defamed.

Gertz v. *Welch*[4] contains the most often quoted definitions of public figures; it classifies them into three types. The involuntary public figure who engages in no purposeful action to influence public debate about a controversial issue is a hypothetical, but rare, possibility. Voluntary public figures, in contrast, are persons who "assume special prominence in the resolution of public questions."[5] Two types of voluntary public figures are defined. First, a public figure for "all purposes and in all contexts" achieves "pervasive fame or notoriety."[6] Secondly, a limited public figure "voluntarily injects himself or is drawn into a particular public controversy and thereby becomes a public figure for a limited range of issues."[7] These categories are explained first, however, in *Curtis Publishing Co.* v. *Butts*.[8]

Another important, but too often overlooked, aspect of the public figure concept has roots in the Sedition debates:

---

[3]403 U.S. 29 (1971).
[4]418 U.S. 323 (1974).
[5]*Gertz*, 418 U.S. at 351.
[6]*Gertz*, 418 U.S. at 351
[7]*Gertz*, 418 U.S. at 351.
[8]388 U.S. 130 (1967).

distinguishing between the public and private actions of a public servant. This distinction was recognized by Libertarian critics of the 1798 Act, but its first modern formulation can be traced to *Garrison* v. *Louisiana*[9] and later to *Patriot Co.* v. *Roy.*[10] "Of course any criticism of the manner in which a public official performs his duties will tend to affect his private, as well as his public, reputation," Brennan writes in *Garrison*, but, "Anything which might touch on an official's fitness for office is relevant [to the actual malice privilege]."[11] The Court seeks here to preclude converting criticism of public action into personal criticism of a public official because this transmogrification wrongly changes criticism of public actions into a personal attack. The unequivocal and ineluctable implication is that, in the life of public persons, there exists few actions not relevant to fitness for office.

Moreover, since the actual malice privilege requires knowing what reporters believe about the truth of their statements, *Sullivan* eventually results in attempts by lawyers to determine a journalist's state of mind. The standards or levels of fault have also become issues as a result of this case. Lower courts have been forced to draw distinctions between those actions that constitute actual malice and those that constitute lesser forms of fault. The Court makes clear time and time again that mere failure to investigate may constitute negligence, but it does not constitute actual malice. The justices also continually assert that actual malice must be demonstrated with clear and convincing evidence. A mere preponderance of the evidence is insufficient.

Critics of the 1798 Sedition Act asserted that, because fact and opinion were often indistinguishable and because opinions were not provable in a courtroom as true, libelous

---

[9]379 U.S. 64 (1964).
[10]401 U.S. 265 (1971).
[11]*Garrison*, 379 U.S. at 77.

opinions deserve a qualified privilege. Indeed, most jurists believed the Court accepted this idea in 1974 when, in dicta of *Gertz*, it said there is no such thing as a false opinion. Like the 1789 critics, though, the Court faced the problem of defining the concept of opinion. One such definition was promulgated in *Milkovich* v. *Lorain Journal*, Co.,[12] where the Court said, in essence, that the word opinion must be capable of being interpreted as meaning idea before it falls under any limited privilege from punishment for libel. A majority of justices asserted that opinions implying the existence of facts capable of being proved true or false are protected only to the degree that the implied facts are themselves true and nondefamatory. The less opinions rely on a factual basis, therefore, the more likely they are to be eligible for the fair comment defense.

These justices accepted a lower court's list (*Ollman* v. *Evans*[13]) of four criteria that distinguish between fact and opinion: (1)the specific language used; (2) whether the statement is verifiable; (3) the general context of the statement; and (4) the broader context in which the statement appeared. The Court noted that, in addition to statements that meet these criteria, two previously defined categories of opinion also qualify for the fair comment defense: imaginative expression and rhetorical hyperbole. Brennan, in dissent, asserted that a third category should be added: conjecture.

Nor should the Court's avowed rationale be overlooked. Society's pervasive and strong interest in preventing and redressing attacks upon reputation, the majority asserts, must be recognized as a counterbalance to the risks of free and uninhibited discussion of public issues. In short, the Court attempts to balance the value of a single person's reputation against the value of vigorous public debate to all citizens.

---

[12]497 U.S. 1 (1990).
[13]750 F.2d 970 (D.C. Cir. 1984).

Finally, it is worth noting also that this Court takes care to point out that every statement beginning with the words "in my opinion" is not automatically an opinion and so is not necessarily capable of being defended as fair comment.

To the surprise of few jurists, the concept of knowing falsehood created in *Sullivan* continually has eluded precise definition. A recent challenge, for example, focused on using quotation marks. In *Masson* v. *New Yorker*,[14] the Court asserted that journalists constitutionally can change words within quotation marks as long as the change does not alter the basic or substantial meaning of the quotation. Justice White, in dissent, argued that changing a quotation is in itself clear evidence that authors know the words in the resulting creation are false. To suggest that a change in wording must also result in a change in meaning before this change is considered unconstitutional is to suggest, as White sees it, that authors are being given license to lie as long as their lies do not exceed a certain limit. White argued that the Court has given journalists license to attribute to a source words that a person never spoke simply because they cannot remember the exact words of the quotation. If reporters cannot remember the exact words, White asserts, then they should not use quotation marks.

Yet the Court did not go as far in the other direction as Malcolm requested. She pleaded for the notion of a rational interpretation, asking the justices to rule that a quotation passes constitutional muster as long as it is a rational interpretation of what the speaker said. The majority ruled, in contrast, that such a ruling would vitiate the concept of a direct quotation. Quotations are not interpretations, it said, but rather an attempt to recover the exact words spoken by a source. In summary, the court said changing quotations to correct grammar and to improve syntax is constitutional as long as it does not result in changing the essential meaning of the original words.

---

[14]501 U.S. 496 (1991).

In spite of the Court's best efforts, from the very first libel plaintiffs sought to define knowing falsehood as failure to investigate. In *Sullivan* the justices ruled that "the mere presence of the [accurate] stories [that could have corrected the errors of the alleged libelous advertisement] in the files [of the *Times*] does not, of course, establish that the Times "knew" the advertisement was false."[15] That same year, Brennan penned in *Garrison* these oft-quoted words, "Only those false statements made with the high degree of awareness of their probable falsity demanded by New York Times may be the subject of either civil or criminal sanctions."[16]

The first assault on this barrier was led in 1967 by none other than Chief Justice Earl Warren when he asserted in a *Curtis* concurring opinion that the "slipshod and sketchy"[17] conduct of journalists at the *Post* combined with "little investigative effort" constituted a "reckless course"[18] of action. In short, Warren maintained that poor investigative techniques are indeed evidence of reckless disregard for the truth. The three justices who formed the plurality opinion also came up with what some later jurists considered a weakened definition of reckless disregard for the truth: extreme departure from the standards of investigation and reporting ordinarily adhered to by responsible publishers.

The *per curiam* decision of *Beckley Newspapers Corp. v. Hanks,*[19] however, produced an immediate reaffirmation of the *Sullivan* standard. Here the Court asserts unequivocally that a newspaper's failure to investigate falls far short of the "'high degree of awareness of . . . probable falsity demanded by New York Times.'"[20] The next year White asserts in *St. Amant* v.

---

[15]*N.Y. Times*, 367 U.S. at 287.
[16]*Garrison*, 379 U.S. at 74.
[17]*Curtis*, 388 U.S. at 160.
[18]*Curtis*, 388 U.S. at 170.
[19]389 U.S. 81 (1967).
[20]*Beckley*, 389 U.S. at 85.

Thompson[21] that reckless conduct is not measured by whether a reasonably prudent person would investigate before publishing. In place of the *Garrison* notion positing "a high degree of awareness of probable falsity,"[22] White substitutes the idea that actual malice means journalists must entertain "serious doubts"[23] about the truth of their words.

Even as he defends the strong barriers to overcoming the requirements of actual malice, however, White notes their shortcomings. He writes, "It may be said that such a test puts a premium on ignorance, encourages the irresponsible publisher not to inquire, and permits the issue to be determined by the defendant's testimony that he published the statement in good faith and unaware of its probable falsity."[24] He admits that "recklessness may be found where there are obvious reasons to doubt . . . accuracy."[25]

Abe Fortas in his dissenting opinion supports Warren's lowered concept of recklessness. For him, mere failure to check on the reliability of sources who make defamatory statements is adequate evidence of reckless disregard for the truth. Journalists, he asserts, have a duty to check the reliability of libelous statements.[26]

The most recent resolution of this issue can be found in *Harte-Hanks Communications, Inc.* v. *Connaughton.*[27] Although the Court specifically and emphatically rejected the 1967 *Curtis* notion of "extreme departure from the standards of investigation and reporting ordinarily adhered to by responsible publishers,"[28] it also said that purposely avoiding an

---

[21]390 U.S. 727 (1968).
[22]*Garrison*, 379 U.S. at 74.
[23]St. Amant, 390 U.S. at 729.
[24]St. Amant, 390 U.S. at 731.
[25]St. Amant, 390 U.S. at 732.
[26]St. Amant, 390 U.S. at 734.
[27]491 U.S. 657 (1989).
[28]*Curtis*, 388 U.S. at 155.

investigation is a much more serious wrong than merely failing to investigate. Consequently, a majority of the justices ruled that giving the appearance of purposely avoiding an investigation into a news story can be interpreted constitutionally by a jury to constitute adequate evidence of reckless disregard for the truth.

Although the United States Supreme Court has the last word in a libel case, and even though the First Amendment of the United States Constitution governs all forms of speech and is applied to the states by the Fourteenth Amendment, libel law is primarily state law,[29] so it is necessary now to look at what is unique about Pennsylvania libel law. Pennsylvania libel law, like that of most other states and indeed other countries, is based on the notion that all persons are entitled by "reason and natural justice" to protection of their reputations from damaging and defamatory words. If such words are spoken, then they are termed slander; if written, they are libel.

Most law relevant to media defendants falls under libel. The commonly cited distinction centers on the concept of premeditation. Because slander is spoken, it is thought to be spontaneous and so not as worthy of punishment as premeditated words would be. In addition, spoken words have a short life and ordinarily can reach only as far as the speaker can yell. Written words, in contrast, require prior thought and so are believed to be more worthy of punishment because they are the result of advance plotting and represent a deliberate attempt to defame.

Because of modern technology, some of the distinctions between libel and slander have been blurred. Certainly, radio

---

[29]"Although a defamation suit has profound First Amendment implications, it is fundamentally a state cause of action." *McDowell v. Paiewonsky*, 769 F.2d 942, 945 (3d Cir. 1985). "Although replete with First Amendment implications, a defamation suit fundamentally is a state cause of action." *Marcone v. Penthouse International Magazine for Men*, 754 F.2d 1072, 1077 (3d Cir. 1985).

and television broadcasts can reach as many persons as can a newspaper or magazine article. Moreover, sound recording technology has given spoken words a life nearly as long as written words. Consequently, although words may be spoken on television and radio broadcasts, they fall in the category of libel, not slander.

Even though Pennsylvania statutes related to libel are extremely brief, they do provide convenient organizational guidelines. They prescribe, for example, what persons who feel libeled must prove in order to win a law suit. This list consists of seven items.

(1) The defamatory character of the communication.
(2) Its publication by the defendant.
(3) Its application to the plaintiff.
(4) The understanding by the recipient of its defamatory meaning.
(5) The understanding by the recipient of it as intended to be applied to the plaintiff.
(6) Special harm resulting to the plaintiff from its publication.
(7) Abuse of a conditionally privileged occasion.[30]

Pennsylvania statues, likewise, list three items that an accused libeler bears the burden of proving. These items constitute, in effect, defenses.

(1) Until a 1980 United States Supreme Court decision, defendants were required in Pennsylvania to prove the truth of a defamatory communication.[31] Today, this burden must be born by persons who wish to prove they were libeled.
(2) The privileged character of the occasion on which it was published.

---

[30]42 Pa.Cons.Stat.Ann. § 8343 (2002).
[31]*Philadelphia Newspapers, Inc. v. Hepps*, 475 US 767 (1980).

(3) The character of the subject matter of defamatory comment as of public concern.[32]

The burden of proof may shift, though, as a libel case proceeds. Persons who feel libeled have the burden to prove first that the statement complained of was defamatory, false, and that it identified them. The burden then shifts to the accused libeler to show that the statement is protected by some sort of privilege, such as truth or fair comment. Finally, the burden shifts back to the persons who feel libeled to show that the privilege was abused.

A good way to understand Pennsylvania libel law, consequently, is to examine in more detail these ten items related to burdens of proof. Plaintiff burdens one and four are discussed in the section devoted to defamation; three and five in the section devoted to identification; two is found under communication; seven in privilege, and six in damages. The plaintiff's burden of truth constitutes a separate section. Separate sections are also devoted to the defendant's two burdens of showing privilege or fair comment.

Defamatory Character of Statements

According to Pennsylvania statute, the first item that must be proved by persons who feel libeled is the defamatory character of an allegedly libelous statement. The first test for libel, therefore, is simply determining if the words are capable of injury.[33] No injury, no libel.

To reach the level of defamation, the hurt or pain of libelous words must result in more than mere embarrassment or

---

[32]42 Pa.Cons.Stat.Ann. § 8343 (2002).
[33]*Corabi* v *Curtis Publishing Co.,* 273 A.2d 899 (Pa. 1971); "The threshold issue . . . is whether or not the communication in question is capable of a defamatory meaning"; *Petula* v *Mellody,* 588 A.2d 103, 105 (Pa.Commw.1991); *Goralski* v *Pizzimenti,* 540 A.2d 595 (Pa.Commw. 1988); *Thomas Merton Center* v. *Rockwell International Corp.,* 442 A.2d 213 (Pa. 1981).

annoyance.[34] Perhaps the most widely accepted definition can be found in *Restatement of Torts*. This definition--although containing sexist and some would say racist (blacken) language--often has been quoted with approval by the Pennsylvania Supreme Court: "A libel is a maliciously written or printed publication which tends to blacken a person's reputation or to expose him to public hatred, contempt, or ridicule, or to injure him in his business or profession."[35] The Pennsylvania Superior Court in June of 2000 provided this definition of defamation:

> A communication is defamatory if it tends to harm the reputation of another as to lower him in the estimation of the community or to deter third persons from associating or dealing with him. A communication is also defamatory if it ascribes to another conduct, character or a condition that would adversely affect his fitness for the proper conduct of his proper business, trade or profession.[36]

In short, a person must suffer damage that a court can provide compensation for. Journalists usually cannot be taken into

---

[34]*McAndrew* v. *Scranton Republican*, 72 A.2d 780 (Pa. 1950). Under Pennsylvania law, the court must decide at the outset whether a statement is capable of defamatory meaning. *Tucker v Fischbein*, 237 F.3d 275, 281 (3d Cir. 2001). See also *Thomas Merton Ctr. v. Rockwell Int'l Corp.*, 442 A.2d 213, 215-16 (Pa. 1981). "We recognize that the issue of determining whether the alleged defamatory publication is a "mere annoyance or embarrassment" on the one hand, or sufficient to establish "personal humiliation and mental anguish and suffering" on the other hand is sometimes difficult. The difference between these two standards appears to be a matter of degree." *Tucker* 796 A.2d at 16.

[35]*Corabi*, 273 A.2d at 904; *see also Baker v Lafayette College*, 532 A.2d 399, 402 (Pa. 1987); *Thomas Merton Center* v. *Rockwell International Corp.*, 442 A.2d 213, 215 (Pa. 1981).

[36]*Tucker v. Philadelphia Daily News*, 757 A.2d 938, 942 (Pa.Super. 2000).

court for libeling the dead, therefore, because dead persons do not suffer when their reputations are lowered (or at least they are not aware of the consequences of a tainted reputation) and you cannot compensate the dead (or at least they are incapable of enjoying the compensation).

In one case, a fired employee said a company manager falsely attributed this statement to her, "You better play ball with me, or I'm going to put your f--king head through the wringer with your extramarital affair."[37] She sued the manager, saying that he libeled her when he falsely claimed she said these words. The court said attributing the words to her clearly embarrassed her, but they did not lower the community's estimation of her. Indeed, it said alleging that someone is crude, vulgar and insubordinate is not as offensive as other statements which have been characterized as incapable of defamatory meaning. Among the other nondefamatory statements noted by the court are these: was uncooperative, took an adversarial position, was crazy, lacked confidence in the employee's work performance, lacked trust in, and was terminated due to misconduct. The court also held that a cartoon portraying a person as vile, obscene, abusive insensitive, and paranoid was no defamatory.[38] It is important to note, however, that a statement published to an employee's supervisor and co-workers saying the employee opened company mail was ruled defamatory because it implied the employee had committed a crime. [39]

There are two steps to determining whether words are defamatory, each made during a civil procedure by a different person. First, after someone files a libel suit, a judge determines if the alleged words are capable of satisfying the

---

[37] *Maier v. Maretti*, 671 A.2d 701, 701 (Pa.Super. 1995)

[38] *Wecht v. PG Publishing Co.*, 510 A.2d 769, 772 (Pa.Super. 1986).

[39] *Rybas v. Wapner*, 457 A.2d 108, 110 (Pa.Super. 1983).

legal definition of defamation.[40] The judge must examine the meaning of the allegedly defamatory statement in its full context[41] and then evaluate "the effect [it] is fairly calculated to produce, [and] the impression it would naturally engender in the minds of the average persons among whom it is intended to circulate."[42] Although it is not enough that the offending statement is merely embarrassing or annoying,[43] a court should not dismiss a charge of libel unless it is "clear that the publication is incapable of a defamatory meaning."[44] If a judge feels the words are not capable of a defamatory meaning, then that judge rules the words not libelous according to the law.[45] The case is dismissed, and the only recourse left to persons who feel libeled is an appeal.

Consequently, the second step is never reached when a judge rules the words do not fit the law's definition of libel. For example, when a candidate for political office filed a libel suit because he felt libeled by a newspaper that accused him of changing political parties just before an election, a judge ruled that the words constituting such an accusation are not libelous according to the legal definition, whether or not they are true. Thus, reporters may report this fact about candidates for political office in Pennsylvania and not fear losing a libel suit.

---

[40]"In the first instance, the Court must determine whether the defendant has injured the plaintiff's reputation under the applicable state law. If so, then the Court must ascertain whether the First Amendment nevertheless prohibits the imposition of liability." *Steaks Unlimited, Inc. v. Deaner*, 623 F.2d 264, 270 (3d Cir. 1980). *See also Marcone* v. *Penthouse Intern. Magazine for Men*, 754 F.2d 1072 (1985).

[41]*See Beckman v. Dunn*, 419 A.2d 583, 586 (Pa. Super. 1981).

[42] Corabi, 273 A.2d at 907.

[43]See *Bogash v. Elkins*, 176 A.2d 677, 678 (Pa. 1962).

[44]*Vitteck v. Washington Broad. Co.*, 389 A.2d 1197, 1200-01 (Pa. Super. 1978).

[45]*Brophy* v. *Philadelphia Newspapers, Inc.*, 422 A.2d 625, 628 (Pa. Super. 1980).

A second step is required, however, after a judge declares the words at issue may be--not necessarily are--libelous according to law.[46] This declaration does not mean the words have been ruled legally libelous. Rather, it means only that a judge feels it is possible for reasonable persons to view the words as libelous. The theoretical second step, therefore, is that reasonable persons must be given a chance to decide whether the words are libelous in fact. In actual practice, a jury represents the reasonable persons who take the second step by making this factual decision.[47]

To summarize, after a judge determines that the words at issue could fall within the legal definition of libel (determines the law), then a jury determines whether the words are libelous in fact (determines the fact). Thus, words are libelous only when a judge and jury declare them to be libelous. Even though words claimed to be defamatory are to be understood in their plain and natural meaning, it is impossible, even for the most sophisticated social scientists, to predict what judges and juries will decide they mean in law or in fact. This procedure can result in some discomfort and apprehension for journalists. Reporters may be hesitant to use the best and most accurate words because they fear a jury someday may declare them libelous.

It is possible, however, to know in advance whether some words are in themselves libelous; that is, if they are libelous per se (by themselves or intrinsically). Certain words have been declared by Pennsylvania courts to be libelous in themselves without proof of special damages. The most commonly cited examples are words falsely imputing the

---

[46]If the court determines that the statement is capable of a defamatory meaning, the jury must then decide whether the recipient actually understood the statement to be defamatory." *Tucker v Fischbein*, 237 F.3d 275, 282 (3d Cir. 2001). *See Corabi* 273 A.2d at 904.

[47]*Gordon* v. *Random House, Inc.*, 349 F. Supp. 919 (E.D. Pa. 1972).

commission of a crime, an arrest, a conviction, or imprisonment. It is particularly dangerous to impute falsely the commission of a crime involving moral turpitude. Examples declared defamatory by the courts are the following: adultery, beating a spouse, arson, forgery, perjury, and receiving stolen goods.[48] In addition, a court said the following words are capable of a defamatory meaning because they can be interpreted reasonable to suggest that the person described is an arson suspect: "Matt . . . burned down the cabin."[49] Asserting loathsome diseases, business misconduct, in competency in a profession have also been ruled libelous per se.[50]

Words not in this list cannot be used carelessly, though, because a jury may be allowed to consider words anew when they are used in a different context. Words may also, by extension, lose their defamatory force. For example, during the 1950's it was ruled libelous per se to call someone a communist, and no less than six Pennsylvania law school journal articles discussed this topic from 1950 through 1957.[51] Yet in 1964 the Pennsylvania Supreme Court ruled that the words "Communist tendencies" were not libelous.[52] In 1897 the Pennsylvania Superior Court said it was libelous to assert a person "came from a disreputable and dishonest family,"[53] but calling a married woman "Scotch bitch," "bastard," and "bum" was ruled not sufficiently insulting to sink to the level of defamation.[54]

---

[48]*Pennsylvania Law Encyclopedia*, p. 232.
[49]*Sokoloski* v. *Tirpak*, 51 Luz.L.Reg. 51 (1961).
[50]*Chicarella* v. *Passant*, 494 A.2d 1109, 1114 (Pa. Super 1985).
[51]*Solosko* v. *Paxton*, 383 Pa. 419 (1956); 18 *University of Pittsburgh Law Review* 424 (1957); 60 *Dickinson Law Review* 354 (1956); 1 *Villanova Law Review* 363 (1956); 14 *University of Pittsburgh Law Review* 624 (1953); 98 *University of Pennsylvania Law Review* 931 (1950); 24 *Temple Law Review* 247 (1950.
[52]*Clark* v. *Allen*, 204 A.2d 42 (Pa. 1964).
[53]*Walter* v. *Erdman*, 4 Pa.Super.Ct. 348 (1897).
[54]*Halliday* v. *Cienkowski*, 3 A.2d 372 (Pa. 1939).

When a court is seeking to determine whether a communication could be understood as defamatory, it is not required to find the communication to have caused actual harm to reputation; it need only look to the general tendency of the words to have such an effect.[55] When C. Delores Tucker--a nationally known and outspoken advocate for the black community, who, in 1993, became a leader in a movement against gangsta rap--and her husband William Tucker filed a libel suit claiming, among other damages, a lost of consortium, the *Philadelphia Daily News* reported that they were claiming damages to their sex life, which is only one component of the legal definition of loss of consortium. The Tuckers said the emphasis in the articles on only one possible component of a loss of consortium claim, to the exclusion of the other ingredients, created an impression that would expose them to public hatred and ridicule. The Pennsylvania Superior Court agreed and ruled that, because of their advanced age and their reputation as people of strong morals, the suggestion in the newspaper articles that they are overly concerned with sexual matters could be capable of defamatory meaning.[56]

While it is not defamatory to call a person a bigot or any other name descriptive of political, racial, religious, economic, or sociological philosophies or memberships,[57] asserting that an employee left employment without giving notice was ruled defamatory[58] as was connecting a person with illicit drug transactions.[59] In addition, headlines are to be considered when evaluating whether a news story is libelous.[60]

---

[55]*Agriss v. Roadway Exp., Inc.*, 483 A.2d 456, 461 (Pa. Super.Ct. 1984).
[56]*Tucker v. PNI*, 757 A.2d 938 (Pa.Super.Ct. 2000).
[57]*Rybas v. Wapner*, 457 A.2d 108 (Pa.Super.Ct. 1983).
[58]*Birl v. Philadelphia Electric Co.*, 167 A.2d 472 (Pa. 1961).
[59]*Marcone v. Penthouse International Magazine For Men*, 484 U.S. 864 (1985).
[60]*Mengel v. Reading Eagle Co.*, 88A. 660 (Pa. 1913).

Pennsylvania statutes assert that another important aspect of testing for defamatory meaning is the understanding of the words by a recipient. This aspect is based on the proposition that the reputation of a person is lowered only when other persons hearing an allegedly libelous statement understand the meaning of that statement to be defamatory. According to statute, persons who feel libeled bear the burden of showing that the audience understood a statement to be defamatory. The law focuses upon the receiver here. Consequently, in this test, the writer's intentions do not affect the perceived meaning of the words.[61]

The point is not what the writer intended the words to mean, but what the audience reasonably would take them to mean.[62] Illustrative of the case law on this point is this statement:

> To determine the meaning of an [allegedly libelous] article it must be read in the context of all the other words. The test being the effect which the article is fairly calculated to produce an impression, which it would naturally engender in minds of average persons among whom it is intended to circulate, and words must be given by judges and juries same signification that other people are likely to attribute to them. [63]

Pennsylvania courts have ruled repeatedly that the "nature of the audience hearing the remarks is a key factor in considering whether they are capable of defamatory

---

[61]*Corabi v. Curtis Pub. Co.*, 273 A.2d 899 (Pa. 1971).
[62]*Baird v. Dun & Bradstreet*, 285 A.2d 166 (Pa. 1971).
[63]*MacRae v. Afro-American Co.*, 172 F.2d 287 (3d Cir. 1959). When determining whether a publication is capable of a defamatory meaning, the court must consider the impression that the entire article would engender in the minds of the average reader. *Green v. Mizner*, 692 A.2d 169, 172 (Pa. Super.Ct. 1997).

meaning."[64] Time magazine, for example, won a libel case by asserting that, since its audience was "far more sophisticated and intelligent than an average reader," its readers would recognize that a discription of the damage caused by an errant golf ball was not defamatory.[65] Likewise, a federal court ruled that the meaning of words used in a television newscast must be defined by determining what the television audience would take them to mean.[66]

Words also may be ruled libelous when an audience mistakenly understands the words to be defamatory as long as a jury feels the audience reasonably inferred a defamatory meaning.[67]

While it is true that, according to case law, the meaning of a statement is determined by those persons who are members of the audience to which the statement is directed, nevertheless, ultimately a judge or a jury decides what meaning a member of that audience in fact would give to a particular statement. Since it is often impossible to poll the members of a given audience, the more-than-a-little-complex task of the jury, in effect, is to determine whether an allegedly libelous statement is defamatory by inferring what a particular audience would believe the words mean.

Identification

According to Pennsylvania statute, another item that persons who feel libeled must prove is that the statements objected to identify them. The second test of libel, therefore, is identification. A person's reputation cannot suffer if no one knows who it is that the libelous words refer to. In contrast, a reputation clearly can be damaged if others mistakenly, but

---

[64]*Fram v. Yellow Cab Co. of Pittsburgh*, 380 F.Supp. 1314 (W.D. PA. 1974) represents an illustrative opinion.
[65]*Sellers v. Time, Inc.,* 400 U.S. 830 (1970).
[66]*Fram*, 380 F.Supp. at 1330.
[67]*Baird v. Dun*, 446 Pa. At 271.

reasonably, conclude that libelous words apply to the wrong person. A writer can libel John, for example, when writing words about Mary if readers reasonably--even if mistakenly-- could conclude that the words were written about John.

The most common mistaken belief about identification, however, is that a name is required in order for an identification to hold up in court. Yet all that is required is that the audience be able to identify the person whom a writer is addressing the words to, whether or not a name is mentioned.

One factor used by the courts to determine identification by means other than a name is the size of a group libeled. While the courts have ruled that a large class or group, such as an entire profession, cannot sue for defamation, if a group is so small that an audience is likely to identify individual members, then an individual member can sue. In other words, if the group is small enough so that members of an audience reasonably could conclude that a particular person is being referred to, then a writer has identified that person merely by referring to the group the person belongs to. Moreover, if the group is small, writers cannot escape liability by using the phrases "a number of," "some of," or "one of."[68]

Calculating a number to represent the border between large and small is extremely difficult; courts have varied roughly between 25 and 100. So, if journalists libel a group comprising a small enough number of persons--such as, say, 25- -then they have identified everyone and anyone in that group and so libeled each and every member merely by naming the group.

For example, a court allowed a commissioner to sue a newspaper when a reporter wrote that the District Attorney's of- fice was investigating a report that a number of township commissioners were involved in a corrupt transaction and that all 13 commissioners would be questioned. The Court asserted

---

[68] *Farrell v. Triangle Publications, Inc.*, 159 A.2d 734 (Pa. 1960).

that the article was defamatory and that the commissioner was sufficiently identified.[69]

It is also possible that others may conclude journalists have referred to only one particular person in the group, even though they identified by name only the group itself.[70] The essential point is whether or not the particular person bringing the suit can be identified by a reference made to a group.[71]

Communication

Although journalists may have written or uttered defamatory words about someone they clearly identified, they have not yet necessarily committed libel. Pennsylvania statute requires persons who feel libeled to prove that the defamation was communicated.[72] The third test, then, is communication to a third party. There are two parts to this test: identifying the sender and identifying the receiver of the libelous statement.

For journalists, identifying the sender usually means ascribing responsibility. If a reporter for a weekly newspaper writes a libelous news story, for example, then a question is raised concerning whether the news editor, the managing editor, the publisher, or the operator of the printing press also are responsible to some degree. Much of the answer is found in the notion of "respondeat superior."

Respondeat superior is a legal doctrine asserting that masters are liable in certain cases for the wrongful acts of their servants. This doctrine usually limits the liability to acts

---

[69]*Farrell v. Triangle Publications, Inc.*, 159 A.2d at 738. See also *Thompson* v. *Farley*, 35 D. & C.2d 157 (1964) . Where a defamatory statement is directed toward a comparatively small class or group all of whose constituent members may be readily identified and recipients of defamatory matter are likely to identify some of individual members of the group an individual member of group may sue for damages done his reputation thereby.

[70]Class defamation, *see* 6 *Vill.L.Rev.* 525 (1961).

[71]*Farrell* v. *Triangle Publications, Inc.*, 159 A.2d 734, 736 (Pa. 1960).

[72]42 Pa.Cons.Stat.Ann. § 8343.

committed during the servant's scope of employment. The United States Supreme Court found Forest City Publishing Company liable under the traditional doctrine of respondeat superior, for example, when a reporter within the scope of his employment at a newspaper invaded the privacy of a person about whom he wrote a news story.[73]

Broadcasters have a special interest in the problem of assigning responsibility because they may have no control over who issues statements over their airwaves. Pennsylvania law specifically addresses this issue and exempts "owners, licensees, and other operators of any . . . radio and television station or network" from responsibility for libelous statements broadcast outside their control.[74]

The media have a particular problem with communication because a new charge of libel can be instituted each time a libelous statement is repeated. Thus a newspaper publishing 100,000 copies theoretically could be facing 100,000 counts of libel. To address this issue, the legislature passed the Uniform Single Publication Act.[75] In essence, this law states that a single issue of a publication, such as a newspaper, constitutes a single publication, and only one charge of libel can arise from a statement in it, no matter how many copies were circulated.[76]

The courts, however, have qualified the protection from this act. A common misconception is that accurately printing a letter to the editor does not constitute libel. If the letter contains a libelous statement, however, then printing it constitutes repeating the libel. One trial court ruled, moreover, that failure to remove a libelous statement can be considered republication and so constitutes a second instance of libel even though only

---

[73]*Cantrell* v. *Forest City Publishing Company*, 419 U.S. 245 (1974).
[74]42 Pa.Cons.Stat.Ann. § 6791-6780.
[75]42 Pa.Cons.Stat.Ann. § 8341.
[76]*Graham* v. *Today's Spirit*, 468 A.2d 454 (Pa. 1983).

one issue of a newspaper was published.[77]   Finally, the Pennsylvania Supreme Court ruled that a statement published in two newspapers with the same owner constituted more than a single publication.[78]

Identifying the receiver is usually not difficult for journalists. One enterprising small town publisher, though, did present an interesting defense by saying the libel was never communicated because no one read his newspaper. Rarely do media libel suits turn on this point. Private suits, in contrast, are often concerned with this issue. A good rule to keep in mind is the common law notion that a defamation is not considered communicated to a third party if the communicator of a defamation could not have anticipated that someone would have overheard. Nevertheless, communication is an essential ingredient in the libel formula, and a libel suit cannot be won without showing that the defamatory statement in fact was communicated to a third party.

Justification

Journalists may still survive a libel suit even if they fail all three tests by passing either the fourth or fifth, both of which can be described as affirmative defenses. A negative defense results when journalists simply assert they did not commit libel. If the persons who feel libeled meet all their burdens of proof, however, then clearly libel did occur. It would be foolish in such instances to rely on a denial of the act. Journalists who admit libel nevertheless very well may win a libel suit. They can do so by using what is known as an affirmative defense. In libel law, an affirmative defense is usually raised when journalists admit they libeled, but assert that the libel is perfectly acceptable. In short, the law says that, in certain circumstances, you are allowed to communicate certain libelous statements in certain ways. The burden of proof for an

---

[77]*Beisel* v. *Zerbe*, 11 D&C3d 541 (1979).
[78]*Graham*, 468 A.2d at 458; *see also* 42 Pa.Cons.Stat.Ann. § 8341(b).

affirmative defense, though, rests on the shoulders of the admitted libeler.

The substance of an affirmative libel defense is summarized in statute:

> Justification a defense. In all civil actions for libel, the plea of justification shall be accepted as an adequate and complete defense, when it is pleaded, and proved to the satisfaction of the jury, under the direction of the court as in other cases, that the publication is substantially true and is proper for public information or investigation, and has not been maliciously or negligently made.[79]

The relevant parts to statutory justification number three: (1) the libel is true, (2) its content is of legitimate interest to its intended audience, and (3) the admitted libeler did not commit a fault when expressing the libel. The second of these three parts constitutes the core of an affirmative defense. Two primary ones remain effective in this Commonwealth: privilege and fair comment.

Privilege

Pennsylvania law recognizes two kinds of privilege: absolute and conditional. Absolute means that the holder of the privilege is completely immune from a libel suit. One form of absolute privilege is consent. Simply put, some persons willingly may grant a journalist permission to libeled them. If a person were to distribute an otherwise private defamatory statement about himself or herself, then that person, in effect, has consented to being libeled.

The Pennsylvania Superior Court ruled, for example, that an employee could not recover from an employer when a

---

[79] 42 Pa.Cons.Stat.Ann. § 8342.

letter sent to the employee by the employer stating clearly defamatory reasons for discharge was published by the employee, not the employer. The letter said, among other things, "You were terminated from your position . . . because of your very poor employment record. Your record includes engaging in incidents of poor work performance, failing to give a conscientious effort to your position, harassing and coercing another employee, maligning the company and demonstrating a poor attitude."[80] The employee admitted that he did show the letter to his wife, to other relatives, and to prospective employers during interviews, but he claimed that he was "compelled" to reveal the contents of the letter and that the employer should have foreseen this necessity. The court disagreed.

Another form of absolute privilege exists for governmental officials or persons acting in an official public capacity. Judges or attorneys during a trial, for example, are absolutely privileged to communicate defamatory matter. Thus, persons accused of murder cannot sue a prosecutor for libel after a jury declares them not guilty. Husbands and wives enjoy an absolute privilege to exchange libelous statements. The list of absolute privileges does not include, however, a single one ascribed to journalists.

Conditional privileges are granted more commonly to reporters. Journalists focus a great deal of their attention on one special conditional privilege: reports of official proceedings and public meetings.[81] This privilege is conditional or limited

---

[80] *Yetter v. Ward Trucking Corp.*, 585 A.2d 1022, 1023, 1034 (Pa. Super. 1991).

[81] The United States Supreme Court ruled that there is no necessary constitutional privilege for publishing matters of public concern, *Gertz* v. *Welch*, 418 U.S. 323 (1974), but a conditional privilege does exist for official public documents and events. Later the Court ruled, however, that a private person suing the media for libel related to a matter of public concern

because it applies only to subject matter of public concern and only to a fair and accurate reports of these matters. Thus, a report (news story) about a matter of pubic concern that is not (1) fair and (2) accurate constitutes an abuse of this privilege.[82] The privilege is not easily assumed, therefore, because, first, the problem of what reflects legitimate public concern is certainly amorphous and, secondly, the judgment about the fairness and accuracy of a report can be highly subjective.[83] Journalists may find some comfort, however, in learning that the privilege cannot be lost based solely on style or tone;[84] *Time Magazine*, for example, was found innocent of defamation when charged with using a "flippant" and "smart Alecky" style.[85]

Some rough guidelines are available. First, to satisfy the courts, a report need be only "substantially" correct.[86]

---

has to prove a defamatory statement is false. (*Philadelphia Newspapers, Inc. v. Hepps*, 475 U.S. 767 (1986).

[82] A newspaper has a qualified privilege to make a fair and accurate report of judicial proceedings, including reporting on judicial pleadings such as the complaint in the instant case, if the article is not published solely for the purpose of causing harm to the person being reported on. *Binder v. Triangle Publications, Inc.*, 275 A.2d 53, 56 (1971). "The Pennsylvania Supreme Court has recognized that if the account is fair, accurate and complete, and not published solely for the purpose of causing harm to the person defamed, it is privileged and no responsibility attaches, even though information contained therein is false or inaccurate." *Oweida v. Tribune-Review Pub. Co.*, 599 A.2d 230, 233-34 (Pa. Super. 1991)(citations and internal quotation marks and alterations deleted).

[83] This qualified privilege may be overcome by overly embellishing an account of a proceeding. *Binder*, 275 A.2d at 324.

[84]"[a]n action for defamation cannot be premised solely on [the newspaper's] style or utilization of vivid words in reporting a judicial proceeding." *Binder*, 275 A.2d at 327.

[85]*Sellers v. Time Inc.*, 423 F.2d 887 (3d Cir. 1969).

[86]*Sciandra v. Lynett*, 187 A.2d 586 (Pa. 1963). The court ruled here that news stories containing an abridgment of a governmental report was privileged because the articles as a whole were a fair and substantially correct summary of the report and there was no showing that they were published solely for purpose of causing harm to the plaintiff.

Secondly, to be considered fair, the report must not convey an erroneous impression by omitting or misplacing information.[87] Finally, to benefit from this privilege journalists cannot add defamatory words of their own, they cannot impute corrupt motives to the writing of the report or to anyone mentioned in it, and they cannot indict expressly or by innuendo the veracity or integrity of the writer or anyone written about.[88] A reporter's methods used to gather information and writing style used to express it, moreover, does not void the privilege.

Merely showing that an admittedly libelous statement is privileged, however, does not necessarily mean that the accused libeler has won the case by supporting an affirmative defense. Showing privilege merely shifts the burden of proof to the persons who feels libeled to show that the privilege was abused.

Fair comment

Another affirmative defense journalists can assert is called opinion or fair comment. It can be thought of as another kind of conditional privilege. This privilege is conditioned or limited by undisclosed facts. Writers are privileged to proffer a libelous opinion consisting of fair comment, that is, only if the facts upon which the opinion is based are disclosed. If the opinion is based on undisclosed facts, then the privilege is lost. The theory is that giving the facts upon which an opinion is based enables readers to evaluate an opinion for themselves. If such facts are not given, then a reader may be tempted to infer

---

[87]To determine whether the privilege has been overcome, the question becomes whether a reasonable person, comparing the complaint and the article as a whole, could conclude that the article was a fair and accurate rendition of the complaint. *First Lehigh Bank v. Cowen*, 700 A.2d 498, 503 (Pa. Super. 1997). Whether a communication is conditionally privileged is a matter for the court to determine. *Id.* Whether a privilege is abused is a question for the jury; however, the court may rule on the issue if the evidence is so clear that no reasonable person would determine the issue in any way but one. *Id.*

[88]*Restatement (Second) of Torts.*

their existence. For example, calling a physician a quack without giving the facts upon which is based an opinion of the physician's ineptitude encourages readers to assume there exists some unknown facts of malpractice that supporting the opinion.[89]

The law, therefore, recognizes two kinds of opinion: pure and mixed; a mixed opinion in an opinion mixed with facts. Pure opinion occurs when facts and opinions are both stated, but clearly separated. Typically, a writer would set forth a factual statement and then offer an opinion about it. If a columnist, for example, wrote that a physician amputated the wrong foot from a frost-bitten small game hunter, then that columnist could proffer an opinion about the physician's use of judgment in selecting the wrong leg. Calling the physician a jackass for doing such a thing certainly would be covered by the privilege. Using the term mooncalf might not be, though, since it imputes being a fool from birth, therefore implying the existence of unstated facts that may concern the physician's life prior to this particular operation. In is worth noting, though, that calling someone a skunk, hyena, rat, or jackal has been ruled libelous per se.[90]

Sports reporters may be pleased to learn that calling a golfer a "duffer" was ruled fair comment by a federal court.[91] Another federal court ruled that the words "paranoid" and "schizophrenic" must be proved to refer to actual physiological or mental afflictions of a person bringing a libel suit before they are considered defamatory.[92]

Mixed opinion results when an opinion is asserted without giving the facts upon which it is based. An expression

---

[89]*Braig* v. *Field Communications*, 456 A.2d 1366 (Pa. Super 1983).

[90]*Weider* v. *Hoffman*, 238 F.Supp. 437. 439 (M.D. Pa. 1965).

[91]*Sellers* v. *Time, Inc.*, 423 F.2d 887, 891 (3d Cir. 1969).

[92]*Fram* v. *Yellow Cab Co. of Pittsburgh*, 380 F.Supp. 1314, 1329 (W.D. Pa. 1974).

of mixed opinion suggests implicit facts for the simple reason that no facts are stated explicitly. The implication mixes implied facts with declared opinion to produce what jurists call a mixed opinion. When no explicit factual basis is given for an opinion, then, the law asserts, readers may be tempted to draw an inference that there exists implicit or undisclosed facts giving rise to the expression of the opinion. For example, calling someone a thief implies undisclosed facts that this person has stolen something.

It is important to know that from 1974 to 1990 many jurists thought all pure opinion--the first type--was privileged. This impression came from United States Supreme Court Justice Powell, who wrote in *Gertz* v. *Welch*, "Under the First amendment there is no such thing as a false idea."[93] Then 16 years later, in *Milkovich* v. *Lorain Journal, Co.,* Chief Justice William H. Rehnquist wrote, "We do not think this passage from *Gertz* was intended to create a wholesale defamation exemption for anything that might be labeled 'opinion.'"[94] Rehnquist asserted that the traditional protections for opinion are sufficient, and a special privilege from libel prosecution for pure opinion is not necessary.

Rehnquist sees it this way. The first issue is whether the opinion implies undisclosed facts. Determining that means looking for implications that are capable of being proven objectively true or false. If such objectively verifiable implications exist, then these implications are facts. The next issue, therefore, is to determine if a given implication of undisclosed facts is capable of a defamatory meaning. If it is, then the asserted opinion is not privileged because the facts upon which it is based could be defamatory.

Rehnquist accounts for the 16-year error by pointing out that the word opinion was confused with the word idea.

---

[93]*Gertz* v. *Welch.*, 418 U.S. at 339
[94]*Milkovich* v. *Lorain Journal, Co.* 497 U.S. 1, 17 (1990).

Powell's words, Rehnquist explains, were "merely a reiteration of Justice Holmes' classic 'marketplace of ideas' concept."[95] The traditional opinion privilege does not apply to ideas, but to opinions.

Truth

Another form of statutory justification is truth. Truth was known for years as the golden defense because it can be a complete defense. It too can be thought of as a kind of conditional privilege to libel. The only condition or limitation is that the truth must be as complete as the defamation.

Journalists must be aware, however, that truth is distinguished from accuracy. A news account that is an impeccably accurate account of a defamatory statement or event is simply an accurate libel.[96] In addition, since the truth must be as complete as the allegedly libelous statement in order to offer full protection, the truth of a news story must extend to innuendoes, implications, or insinuations arising from it.[97]

Before 1986, Pennsylvania courts used the common-law assumption that statements about presumed upright persons were, logically, presumed false and so defamers had to prove that their accusations were true. Consequently, accused libelers bore the burden of proving their damaging statements about persons of presumed high character were true.[98] The United States Supreme Court shifted this burden in a case that originated in Pennsylvania.[99]

---

[95]*Milkovich*, 497 U.S. at 17.
[96]*Dunlap* v. *Philadelphia Newspapers, Inc.*, 448 A.2d 6 (Pa. Super. 1982). [allocaater denied September 30, 1982]
[97]*Friday* v. *Official Detective Stories, Inc.*, 233 F.Supp. 1021, 1023 (E.D. Pa.1964).
[98]See, e.g., 2 *University of Pittsburgh Law Review* 1 (1935).
[99]Truth is an affirmative defense under Pennsylvania law, see 42 Pa. Const. Stat. Ann. § 8343(b)(1), but the United States Supreme Court has held that a public figure must bear the burden of proving falsity. See *Philadelphia Newspapers, Inc.* 475 U.S. at 776 (holding that "the common law's rule of

The Court placed on private persons defamed by the media when addressing matters of public concern the burden of proving defamatory statements about them are false. It is important to note that the court limited the burden to (1) private persons, (2) who are engaged in matters of public concern, and (3) who had been defamed by the media. The Court also pointed out that the existence of a shield law does not alter the nature of the burden, even though the shield law may make it a bit more difficult to obtain evidence from the media to prove defamatory statements are false. Finally, it should also be noted that the Court did not address the question whether the burden of proving falsity is required of persons suing nonmedia defendants.

Journalists can find some comfort, therefore, in knowing that public persons and private persons engaged in matters of public concern must show a libelous statement in a mass medium is false before they can collect damages from the accused libeler.

Fault

A third aspect of statutory justification is fault. Even when journalists have communicated to a third party a

---

falsity--that the defendant must bear the burden or proving truth--must similarly fall here to a constitutional requirement that the plaintiff bear the burden of showing falsity"); see also *Steaks Unlimited, Inc. v. Deaner*, 623 F.2d 264, 274 n.49 (3d Cir. 1980) (suggesting that Pennsylvania's practice of placing the burden of proving truth on the defendant is probably unconstitutional); Dunlap, 448 A.2d at 13-14. The Supreme Court has explicitly declined to decide whether the plaintiff must prove falsity by a preponderance of the evidence or by clear and convincing evidence. See *Harte-Hanks*, 491 U.S. at 661 n.2 (declining to resolve the issue, but acknowledging disagreement among the circuits). Compare *Firestone v. Time, Inc.,* 460 F.2d 712, 722-23 (5th Cir. 1972) (Bell, C.J., concurring) (arguing for a clear and convincing standard) with *Goldwater v. Ginzburg*, 414 F.2d 324, 341 (2nd Cir. 1969) (suggesting a preponderance of the evidence standard) and *Rattray v. National City*, 51 F.3d 793, 801 (9th Cir. 1995) (adopting Goldwater).

defamatory statement that is not privileged, they are not liable for damages unless they are at fault.

The United States Supreme Court has focused on this issue a number of times. The Court has long used the term "breathing space" to express the idea that some false, unprivileged, defamatory statements must be allowed to exist without penalty to the authors if freedom of speech is to make a significant contribution to the marketplace of ideas.[100] In short, the Court says you must in some way be at fault before you can be penalized for issuing a libelous statement, even though the statement is shown to be false.

Malice

Although the term fault is conspicuously absent from Pennsylvania libel statutes, malice is required by the courts in order to convict a person of libel. Usually thought to be synonymous with malignancy of temper, vengefulness of spirit, or personal prejudice, legal malice is, instead, a concept defined for the most part by a long series of court decisions.

The Commonwealth's highest court asserted in 1963 that malice for purposes of libel is a reckless disregard of another's rights or the absence of reasonable care and diligence to ascertain truth.[101] Later, this court said malice can also be defined as a lack of good-faith belief that one has a right to express the allegedly libelous statement.[102]

The most famous description of malice is the term actual malice, a fault that must be proven by public figures suing for libel. In *New York Times* v. *Sullivan*, the Court said public officials (later expanded to include all public figures and theoretically at least also some private persons caught up in public matters) must prove actual malice to win libel

---

[100]*NAACP* v. *Button*, 371 U.S. 415, 418 (1963).

[101]*Purcell* v. *Westinghouse Broadcasting Co.,* 191 A.2d 662, 667 (Pa. 1963).

[102]*Forman* v. *Cheltenham Nat. Bank*, 502 A.2d 686, 688 (Pa. Super 1985).

damages.[103] Although the term actual malice existed in law for centuries prior to 1964, the Court that year assigned these words special meaning when used in defamation cases. Actual malice means the defamation was published knowing the words were false or with reckless disregard to their truth.

The traditional distinction between actual and expressed malice (in other words, malice in fact on the one hand and implied, constructive, presumed, or imputed malice or malice in law on the other) is fairly straightforward. Historically, actual malice--malice in fact--suggests ill will, malevolence, grudge, spite, wicked intention, or enmity. Implied malice--malice in law--can be described as doing what any person of reasonable intelligence should have known would result in injury to another. Most commonly it is defined as a wrong done without just cause. Both forms of malice, however, have at their core the essential element of willfulness or deliberateness. In actual malice, the deliberateness is said to be clear; in constructive malice, deliberateness is inferred from or presumed by the character--such as the recklessness--of the wrong.

The Court, it appears, combined features of traditional actual malice in fact with features of malice in law to produce a special form of actual malice applicable to the defamation of public figures. Drawing from traditional actual malice the Court defines ill will as knowing defamatory words are false when composing a libelous statement. From traditional implied malice, the Court says malice can be inferred from a reckless disregard for the falsity or truthfulness of words. Combining elements of traditional actual malice and traditional implied malice, then, the Court develops a definition for a special form

---

[103]*New York Times* v. *Sullivan*, 376 U.S. 254, 265 (1964). The first Pennsylvania Supreme court case to affirm the United State Supreme Court's notion of actual malice is
Clark v. Allen, 204 A.2d 42, 44 (1964). See also, *Flagiello*v. *Pennsylvania Hospital* , 208 A.2d 193, 209 (Pa. 1964) (dissent).

of actual malice that public figures must prove with clear and convincing evidence in order to win a libel suit: showing that the words were published knowing they were false or with a reckless disregard for their truth.[104]

The Pennsylvania Supreme Court has created a unique distinction for determining actual malice in this Commonwealth. It ruled that a "good faith," but "unprofessional mistake," does not rise to the level of actual malice.[105] In contrast, a trial court ruled that the words "conceivably" and "apparently" do not necessarily protect communicators from actual malice.[106]

A federal appeals court upheld a ruling that actual malice did not occur when a Pennsylvania newspaper negligently failed to check the accuracy of statements in a political advertisement.[107] Yet, when a radio station spliced together what were termed "disconnected statements and circumstances" to make a news broadcast appear to be a whole, the Pennsylvania Supreme Court ruled that the station acted maliciously.[108] Nor can the fact that the defendant published the defamatory material in order to increase its profits suffice to prove actual malice.[109] The Pennsylvania Superior Court ruled

---

[104]Proving actual malice calls into question the state of mind of the one who published the allegedly defamatory statement. *Raffensberger v. Moran*, 485 A.2d 447, 453 (Pa. Super. 1983) (internal citations and quotation marks omitted). "Reckless disregard, it is true, cannot be fully encompassed in one infallible definition. Inevitably its outer limits will be marked out through case-by-case adjudication." *Tucker v. PNI*, 757 A.2d at 945.

[105]*Curran* v. *Philadelphia Newspapers, Inc.*, 546 A.2d 639, 650 (Pa. Super.1988).

[106]*Beimel* v. *Peterson*, 18 D & C3d 750, 762 (1981).

[107]*Baldine* v. *Sharon Hearld Co.*, 291 F.2d 703 (3d Cir. 1966).

[108]*Purcell* v. *Westinghouse Broadcasting Co.*, 191 A.2d 662, 669 (Pa. 1963).

[109] *Reiter v. Manna*, 647 A.2d 562, 567 (Pa. Super. 1994). (quoting *Harte-Hanks Communications, Inc. v. Connaughton*, 491 U.S. 657, 666-67,(1989)).

that persons bringing libel actions from a labor dispute must show actual malice.[110]

The definition of a public figure is a bit amorphous, but journalists may wish to know that police officers and candidates for office have been ruled public figures by Pennsylvania courts.[111]

Negligence

Private persons must prove a lower level of fault: negligence. Malice arises from purpose, while negligence arises from an absence of purpose. The characteristic feature of negligence, as distinguished from malice, is inadvertence or absence of an intent to injure. Perhaps the most common definition of negligence is not doing what a reasonably prudent person would do. In defamation, the Court has ruled that negligence means not practicing the standards of reporting ordinarily adhered to by reasonable journalists.[112] If, when communicating to a third party a defamatory statement that is not privileged, a journalist is at fault, then the journalist may have to pay damages, the penalty for losing a libel suit, when an injury resulted from the communication.

Retractions do not constitute an affirmative defense to defamation, but they can be used as an affirmative defense to mitigate damages.[113]

Damages

The area of damages is complex and court decisions--although based on *stare decisis*--often appear inconsistent. The primary reason for these discrepancies is, without doubt, the difficulty of assessing damages arising from libel. Indeed,

---

[110]*Raffensberger* v. *Moran*, 485 A.2d 447 (Pa. Super.1984).

[111]*Stickney* v. *Chester County Communications, Ltd.*, 522 A.2d 66 (Pa. Super. 1987) and *Clark* v. *Allen*, 204 A.2d 42 (Pa. 1964).

[112]*Curtis Publishing Co.* v. *Butts*, 388 U.S. 130 (1967).

[113]*Rossi* v. *McDonnell*, 18 D&C2d 550 (1960).

some persons would argue that such damages are so amorphous and tenuous that they are not worthy of compensation at all.

Nevertheless, there are three traditional justifications for awarding damages to persons who have been libeled.[114] The first is an effort to compensate victims for injury to their reputations, for their consequent financial losses, and for any emotional distress they may have suffered. The second is an attempt to vindicate them and aid them in restoring their reputation. Finally, tradition recognizes a need to punish convicted libelers and to dissuade potential ones. One of the few Pennsylvania statutes covering libel is relevant to the area of damages: "In all civil actions for libel, no damages shall be recovered unless . . . the publication has been maliciously or negligently made."[115]

Pennsylvania, like most states, recognizes two primary kinds of civil damages: general and special. The purpose of general damages is designed to provide compensation for injuries suffered. These damages represent the ordinary, usual, or natural consequences of a civil wrong. Harm or injury to reputation constitutes the specific damage for which libel suits seek compensation. Sometimes general damages are also called presumed damages because in common law general damages traditional have been awarded for harm that is presumed to result from a defamatory statement. In short, persons who are libeled are presumed to have suffered some sort of general injury to their reputations.

Proof of general damages, therefore, is not required when words are libelous per se (in themselves); damage can be presumed from the mere communication of the libel. In short, only the form or nature of injury needs to be proved; the mere existence of damage is assumed. Words imputing a criminal offense, loathsome disease, business misconduct, or serious

---

[114]*Restatement (Second) of Torts §580 (1995).*
[115]42 Pa.Cons.Stat.Ann. § 8344 (2002).

sexual misconduct, for example, have been ruled presumptively damaging.[116]

Victims are entitled to recover, however, only an amount that represents fair compensation for the injury suffered, and the amount of damages must bear some relation to the evidence.[117] A jury may award substantial damages in the millions of dollars for egregious libels or merely nominal damages for an injury it perceives to be minimal. Thus, if a libel severely impeaches a victim's character, then the courts have ruled that substantial damages should be awarded because nominal damages are considered inadequate for such harm.[118] In contrast, only nominal damages are appropriate if the victim did not suffer any actual injury from the publication.[119]

Damages have been declared nominal when "the insignificant character" of the libelous words or of the victim's standing in the community "leads the jury to believe that no substantial harm has been done" to reputation and no other serious harm has resulted from the defamation.[120] For example, a statement asserting a convicted mass murderer was arrested for shoplifting, when no such arrest took place, would elicit no more than nominal damages because, although clearly defamatory, the statement was incapable of injuring whatever goodness remains in the reputation of such a person.

While damage to reputation is extremely subjective, one guideline has been issued. The Pennsylvania Supreme Court ruled that damages to reputation must be based upon the harm the victim suffered "to his reputation within the geographic area where defamatory statement is communicated."[121]

---

[116] *Chicarella* v. *Passant*, 494 A.2d 1109, 1114 (Pa. Super. 1985).

[117] *Altoona Clay Products, Inc.* v. *Dun & Bradstreet, Inc.*, 286 F.Supp. 899, 901 (W.D. Pa. 1968)

[118]First asserted in *Beck* v. *Sitzel*, 21 Pa. 522 (1853).

[119]*Wood* v. *Boyle*, 35 A. 853 (Pa. 1896)

[120] *Restatement (Second) of Torts §620 (1995)*.

[121] *Graham* v. *Today's Spirit*, 468 A.2d 454, 458 (Pa. 1983)

The second form of damages, special harm, is the loss of something having economic or pecuniary value. In addition to the general reputational damages resulting from an injury inflicted by a defamatory statement, a person may show that the words caused particular, verifiable financial loss. This specific loss constitutes special damages that a libeler may be forced to pay.

Whereas general damages are presumed and so, for the most part, do not need to be proved, special damages, which constitute injuries computable in money, require proof, according to Pennsylvania statute,[122] of actual injury.

Examples of special damages are the cost of seeking redress (lawyer's fees, court costs, and the like) and loss of profits, although the courts have ruled that the loss of credit itself is not proof of damages unless it results in a loss of income.[123] It is important to know that a victim's position in life has been considered by the courts relevant to the calculation of money damages suffered.

In 1939 the Pennsylvania Supreme Court ruled that mental distress and consequent physical illness do not constitute special damages and that persons libeled cannot, in any case, recover for nervous shock unaccompanied by physical injuries.[124] Forty-four years later, though, a federal district court ruled that, under Pennsylvania law, libeled persons may recover damages for emotional distress or bodily harm.[125] Because emotional distress is so difficult to measure, juries have awarded arbitrarily high financial penalties.

Punitive damages are called exemplary damages in Pennsylvania. The word exemplary comes from middle

---

[122]42 Pa.Cons.Stat.Ann. § 8344 (2002).

[123]*Altoona Clay Products, Inc.* v. *Dun & Bradstreet, Inc.*, 286 F.Supp. 899, 904 W.D. Pa. 1968). First asserted in *Eckel v. Murphey*, 15 Pa. 488, 495 (1850).

[124]*Halliday* v. *Cienkowski*, 3 A.2d 372, 373 (Pa. 1939).

[125]*Marcone* v. *Penthouse Intern., Ltd.*, 577 F.Supp. 318, 338 (E.D. Pa.1983).

English, and one of its meanings is service as a warning or admonition. The purpose of exemplary damages, therefore, is to punish libelers and to discourage the communication of future defamations. These damages may be awarded only after compensatory damages have been shown or assumed and only if a jury finds actual malice,[126] which the United States Supreme Court defined in 1964 as publishing a libel knowing it is false or with reckless disregard of its truth or falsity.[127]

Just as extenuating circumstance can increase the award of money through exemplary damages, so too can mitigating circumstances decrease it. It is important to remember, though, that mitigating circumstances only reduce damages; they do not constitute a defense in a libel suit. Indeed, the purpose of mitigating evidence, courts have ruled, is not to lend truth to the libel, but rather to show the good intentions of a libeler.

As long ago as 1803 a Pennsylvania court ruled that one legitimate mitigating factor is evidence that a defendant did not originate, but only repeated, the libel,[128] but the Pennsylvania Supreme Court has not ruled on this factor for more than a century.[129] Other mitigating factors accepted by the courts are (1) evidence of a retraction or at least of an offer to give one and (2) evidence showing the bad reputation of the victim.[130] The theory here is that, if a person has a bad reputation to begin with, then libel cannot force it much lower.

Although juries grant the awards, damages must be reasonable, and if a court finds them excessive, it may, and usually does, reduce them. The Pennsylvania Supreme Court asserted more than 50 years ago that persons libeled may collect

---

[126]*Hepps* v. *Philadelphia Newspapers, Inc.,* 475 U.S. 767 (1986).

[127]*New York Times* v. *Sullivan,* 376 U.S. 254 (1964)

[128]*Morris* v. *Duane,* 1 Binn. 90, *Kennedy* v. *Gregory,* 1 Binn. 84, and *Runkle* v. *Myer,* 3 Yates 518.

[129]Not since *Wallace* v. *Rodgers,* 27 A. 163 (Pa. 1893).

[130]*Clark* v. *North American Co.,* 53 A. 237, 254 (Pa. 1902).

only damages that "will fairly compensate" them for the injuries they suffered.[131]

---

[131]*Montgomery* v. *Dennison*, 69 A.2d 520, 526 (Pa. 1949).

Chapter 3

Advertising Law in Pennsylvania

By Kathleen K. Olson

Introduction

Advertising, or "commercial speech," enjoys First Amendment protection, but not to the same degree as other types of expression such as political speech or art. Traditionally advertising received no First Amendment protection, but that changed in 1976 when the U.S. Supreme Court overturned a Virginia statute that prohibited pharmacists from advertising prescription drug prices.[1] The Court in *Virginia State Board of Pharmacy v. Virginia Citizens Consumer Council* ruled that consumers had a First Amendment right to receive certain commercial information so that states could not constitutionally ban even "purely commercial" speech.

While *Virginia State Board of Pharmacy* was a landmark case that granted a certain level of First Amendment status to advertising, commercial speech has remained inferior to other types of speech. False or deceptive advertising and advertising concerning illegal activities, for example, are not protected by the First Amendment and may be banned or otherwise regulated by the government.

---

[1] *Virginia State Board of Pharmacy v. Virginia Citizens Consumer Council*, 425 U.S. 748 (1976).

In 1980, the Court formulated a legal test for courts to use to determine whether governmental restrictions on advertising violate the First Amendment. According to the *Central Hudson* test, the government may regulate non-deceptive advertising only if there is a substantial governmental interest in the regulation, the regulation directly advances that governmental interest, and the regulation is no broader than is needed to further the governmental interest.[2] "The protection available for particular commercial expression," the Court said, "turns on the nature both of the expression and of the governmental interests served by its regulation."[3]

Thus the balancing of government and free-speech interests may depend on the subject matter of the advertising. Advertising for products or services that are legal but considered harmful, such as gambling, tobacco or alcohol, has been given lower speech protection by the Supreme Court in the past. The Court ruled in a 1986 case, for example, that Puerto Rico could ban casinos from targeting their advertising at local residents rather than tourists. The Court ruled that the stated governmental purpose of the ban, which was to minimize the harmful effects of gambling on its own citizens, was substantial enough to justify the regulation.[4] In more recent cases, however, the Supreme Court has reconsidered the status of advertising for harmful products, ruling in 1996 in *44 Liquormart v. Rhode Island* that the state of Rhode Island could not ban liquor advertising despite the argument that the government interest in discouraging alcohol consumption was a legitimate one.[5]

---

[2] *Central Hudson Gas & Electric Corp. v. Public Service Comm'n of New York*, 447 U.S. 557, 564-565 (1980).
[3] *Central Hudson Gas & Electric Corp.*, 563.
[4] *Posadas de Puerto Rico Associates v. Tourism Co. of Puerto Rico*, 478 U.S. 328 (1986).
[5] *44 Liquormart v. Rhode Island*, 517 U.S. 484 (1996).

The *44 Liquormart* ruling required the Pennsylvania Supreme Court to revisit its own decision in a 1994 case in which it had upheld a provision in the Pennsylvania Liquor Code that prohibited liquor licensees from advertising "in any manner whatsoever" the price of alcoholic beverages.[6] The court ruled that the statute was enacted in order to discourage the consumption of alcoholic beverages, which the court found was a legitimate governmental interest. At the same time, the court said, the "careful balancing of competing interests" that is usually required in speech cases was not required here where the acquisition of a liquor license was a privilege and not a constitutional right.[7]

After *44 Liquormart*, however, the Pennsylvania Supreme Court was forced to rehear the case. Because the Pennsylvania statute was "nearly identical" to the Rhode Island statute struck down by the U.S. Supreme Court, the Pennsylvania court reversed course and ruled that the statute violated the First Amendment.[8]

The *Central Hudson* test remains the standard for federal and state courts reviewing the constitutionality of government regulation of advertising. Such regulation is pervasive, as commercial speech is governed by a complicated regulatory scheme that involves state and federal statutes as well as regulatory agencies such as the Federal Trade Commission, the U.S. Postal Service and the Pennsylvania Attorney General's Bureau of Consumer Protection. Advertising regarding specific types of products or services may also be governed by the applicable subject matter agency; for example, the Food and Drug Administration has the authority to regulate advertising for prescription drugs.

---

[6] *Pennsylvania State Police v. Hospitality Investments of Philadelphia*, 650 A.2d 854 (Pa. 1994).

[7] *Pennsylvania State Police*, 856.

[8] *Pennsylvania State Police v. Hospitality Investments of Philadelphia*, 689 A.2d 213 (Pa. 1997).

Advertising law in Pennsylvania

Pennsylvania law includes a myriad of provisions regulating advertising, from prohibitions on the use of the state flag in advertising[9] to identifying who may properly advertise a bingo game.[10] While many advertising provisions can be found alongside regulations governing the advertised products themselves, several general laws exist that are applicable to all types of commercial speech.

The primary statute in Pennsylvania is the Unfair Trade Practices and Consumer Protection Law, which sets out general legal standards applicable to all types of advertising. The Consumer Protection Law makes it illegal to engage in "unfair methods of competition" or "unfair or deceptive acts or practices" in the conduct of commerce. Among the prohibited acts relevant to advertising:

- Passing off one's goods or services as those of another;
- Causing confusion regarding the "source, sponsorship, approval or certification of goods or services" or one's affiliation or association with another;
- Deception regarding the geographic origin of goods or services;
- Representing that a person or goods or services have "sponsorship, approval, characteristics, ingredients, uses, benefits or quantities" that they lack;
- Representing that goods or services are original or new if they are not;
- Representing that goods or services are of a particular standard, quality or grade, or that goods are of a particular style or model, if they are of another;
- Disparaging the goods, services or business of another by false or misleading representations of fact;

---

[9] 18 *Pa.C.S.A* 2102.
[10] Only individuals licensed to conduct bingo games may advertise. 10 P.S. 305(c)(4).

- Advertising goods or services with intent not to sell them as advertised;
- Advertising goods or services with intent not to supply reasonably expectable public demand, unless the advertisement discloses a limitation of quantity;
- Making false or misleading statements of fact concerning the reasons for, existence of, or amounts of price reductions; and
- Engaging in any other fraudulent or deceptive conduct which creates a likelihood of confusion or of misunderstanding.[11]

The Attorney General's office is charged with enforcing the Consumer Protection Law by the use of temporary or permanent injunctions to restrain prohibited acts. The statute also provides for civil penalties of not more than $5,000 for each violation of an injunction issued under the Law.[12] Willful violations of the Law may also be punished by a civil penalty of up to $1,000 per violation. If the victim of a willful violation is over the age of 60, a civil penalty of up to $3,000 per violation may be imposed.[13]

Media outlets that carry a deceptive or fraudulent ad will not be held liable if they accepted the ad in good faith. The Consumer Protection Law does not apply "to any owner, agent or employee of any radio or television station, or to any owner, publisher, printer, agent or employee of a newspaper or other publication, periodical or circular who, in good faith or without knowledge of the falsity or deceptive character thereof, publishes, causes to be published or takes part in the publication of such advertisement."[14] Thus the Pennsylvania Supreme

---

[11] 73 P.S. 201-2.
[12] 73 P.S. 201-8.
[13] 73 P.S. 201-8.
[14] 73 P.S 201-3.

Court held in 1974 that printing companies that had printed unlawful lease forms could not be held liable under the Consumer Protection Law because the printers did nothing more than "perform the mechanical act of setting type" for the landlords who were the main targets of the investigation.[15]

Pennsylvania also makes certain fraudulent business acts criminal offenses, including making "a false or misleading statement in an advertisement addressed to the public or to a substantial segment thereof for the purpose of promoting the purchase or sale of property or services."[16] Violations may be prosecuted as misdemeanors or as felonies if the amount involved exceeds $2,000.[17]

Advertising harmful goods

The U.S. Supreme Court's decision in *44 Liquormart* was followed by several rulings that marked a departure from its earlier analysis regarding advertisement of so-called harmful goods. In *Greater New Orleans Broadcasting Association v. United States*, the Court used the *Central Hudson* test to strike down another ban on casino advertising, saying the government had not made its case that the ban advanced the governmental interest in reducing compulsive gambling.[18] In *Lorillard Tobacco Co. v. Reilly*, the Court struck down a Massachusetts statute that restricted outdoor advertising of smokeless tobacco and cigars.[19] These cases cast into doubt the Court's previous deference to paternal interests set forth by the government as rationales for advertising restrictions. Furthermore, they may signal that Pennsylvania statutes that restrict advertising of

---

[15] *Commonwealth by Creamer v. Monumental Properties, Inc.*, 329 A.2d 812, 827-828 (Pa. 1974).
[16] 18 *Pa.C.S.A.* 4107(a)(5). Another provision of the statute prohibits false statements in the sale of securities. See 18 *Pa.C.S.A.* 4107(a)(7).
[17] 18 *Pa.C.S.A* 4107 (a.1).
[18] *Greater New Orleans Broadcasting Association v. United States*, 527 U.S. 173 (1999).
[19] *Lorillard Tobacco Co. v. Reilly*, 533 U.S. 525 (2001).

harmful products are also vulnerable to constitutional challenge. Those statutes are described below:

Cigarettes

It is unlawful for a dealer to advertise cigarettes for sale at less than cost "with the intent to injure competitors or destroy or substantially lessen competition."[20] A dealer may match a competitor's price in his ads as long as the competitor's price is not artificially low due to bankruptcy or other circumstances.[21]

Drug paraphernalia

It is illegal to place an ad if one knows or has reason to know that the purpose of the ad, in whole or in part, is to promote the sale of objects "designed or intended for use as drug paraphernalia."[22] Violation of the provision is a misdemeanor and is punishable by a fine of up to $2,500 or imprisonment for up to a year, or both.

Pornography

Pennsylvania law prohibits the advertisement of legally obscene materials or information "directly or indirectly stating or purporting to state where, how, from whom, or by what means any obscene materials can be purchased, obtained or had."[23] Advertising for non-obscene adult entertainment clubs is not restricted by this statute, however. In addition, unsolicited e-mail advertising that contains "explicit sexual materials" (sexual depictions that are considered harmful to

---

[20] 72 P.S. 217-A.

[21] 72 P.S. 221-A.

[22] 35 P.S. 780-113(a)(34).

[23] 18 *Pa.C.S.A.* 5903(a)(4). Materials are obscene if the average person applying contemporary community standards would find that the subject matter taken as a whole appeals to the "prurient interest," the subject matter depicts or describes in a patently offensive way, sexual conduct of a type described by the Pennsylvania obscenity statute, and the subject matter, taken as a whole, lacks serious literary, artistic, political, educational or scientific value. 18 *Pa.C.S.A.* 5903(b).

minors) is prohibited unless the sender includes the term "ADV-ADULT" at the beginning of the subject line of the e-mail message.[24]

Alcohol

The Liquor Code regulates alcohol advertising in Pennsylvania. It prohibits not only false or deceptive ads but ads that contain statements "disparaging of the products of a competitor."[25] It also makes it unlawful to advertise a particular brand of alcohol without having on hand and for sale a sufficient quantity to meet normal demands.[26]

Among the more constitutionally vulnerable statutory provisions are those that seek to protect minors from the effects of alcohol advertisements. For example, no print advertisements for alcoholic beverages are permitted within 300 feet of a church, school or public playground, and alcohol ads may not target minors.[27] The Liquor Code goes much further than protection of minors may warrant, however, when it prohibits the advertising of alcohol by mail or by circulars or handbills to the general public and states that an advertisement for alcoholic beverages "shall not be inconsistent with the spirit of safety or safe driving programs."[28]

Finally, Pennsylvania law states that no alcohol advertisements are permitted "either directly or indirectly," in "any booklet, program book, yearbook, magazine, newspaper, periodical, brochure, circular or other similar publication published by, for or in behalf of any educational institution."[29] While this provision was directed at advertisers, it was challenged in federal court by the staff of *The Pitt News*, the student-run newspaper at the University of Pittsburgh. The

---

[24] 18 *Pa.C.S.A.* 5903(a.1).
[25] 47 P.S. 4-498(b).
[26] 47 P.S. 4-493(5).
[27] 47 P.S. 4-498(e).
[28] 47 P.S. 4-498(e).
[29] 47 P.S. 4-498(e)(5).

students argued that the prohibition on alcohol advertising violated their First Amendment rights because it reduced the newspaper's advertising revenue and therefore restricted the number of pages the newspaper could put out. The trial judge threw the case out on the ground that the students had not suffered a direct violation of their constitutional rights and therefore did not have standing to sue.

On appeal, the Third Circuit Court of Appeals found that the students did have standing to sue based on their own First Amendment rights but ultimately ruled that their revenue loss was "nothing more than an incidental economic effect of a regulation aimed at closely regulated third parties."[30]   The content of the student newspaper was not directly restricted by the Liquor Code, the court held, because the paper could seek advertising from many sources, including from "purveyors of alcoholic beverages," as long as alcohol was not mentioned in the ads themselves.

---

[30] *Pitt News v. Fisher*, 215 F.3d 354, 366 (3d Cir. 2000), *cert. denied*, 531 U.S. 1113 (2001).

Chapter 4

Privacy

By Douglas S. Campbell

Alan F. Westin assets that virtually all animals seek periods of time when they desire the company of other animals and other times when they seek individual seclusion.[1] Most social scientists agree that human beings in all cultures, although innately social, desire a minimum amount of privacy because they cannot tolerate extended physical contact with other humans.[2] Darhl Pederesen identified six types of privacy. Reserve is an unwillingness to be with others. Isolation is a desire to be alone and away from others. Solitude is being alone and away from the observation of others. Intimacy with family is the desire to be alone with member's of one's own family. Intimacy with friends is the desire to be alone with one's closest friends, and anonymity is the desire to go unnoticed in a crowd.[3]

A heightened concern over privacy did not arise, however, until the industrial age when persons worked long hours in factories in close quarter with others, when they lived close to each other in urban areas, and, equally important, when information about others became readily available in the mass media. A recognition of a legal right to privacy is commonly traced to the erudite, nineteenth century Judge Thomas

---

[1] *Privacy and Freedom*. New York: Athenaeum, 1967.

[2] Judee K. Burgoon, *A communication model of personal space violations: Explication and initial test*, 4 Human communication research, 124 (1978).

[3] Darhl M. Pederson, *Dimensions of privacy*, 48 Perceptual and motor skills, 1291-1297 (1979).

McIntyre Cooley, who, in the first edition of his law text on torts, coined the phrase the "right to be let alone."[4] Such a concept was objectionably foreign to many Americans who believed this country was founded on the principle that all other persons eagerly welcomed our opinions and ideas and that it was out of social conflict as well as social intercourse that truth and progress arose.

Nevertheless, twelve years later, Louis Brandeis and Samuel D. Warren wrote the first treatise on the right to privacy.[5] They asserted:

> The intensity and complexity of life, attendant upon advancing civilization, have rendered necessary some retreat from the world, and man, under the refining influence of culture, has become more sensitive to publicity, so that solitude and privacy have become more essential to the individual; but modern enterprise and invention have, though invasions upon his privacy subjected him to mental pain and distress, far greater that could be inflicted by mere bodily injury.[6]

Warren and Brandeis proposed limits to this right, recognizing the importance of the free flow of information to a democracy:

> The right to privacy does not prohibit any publication of matter which is of public or general interest.[7] There are those who, in varying degrees, have renounced the right to live their lives screened from public observation. In general, then, the matters of which the

---

[4]Thomas McIntyre Colley, A Treatise on the law of torts or the wrongs which are independent of contract. Chicago 29 (1878).

[5] "The Right to Privacy," 4 *Harvard Law Review 193*.

[6] Warren, 196.

[7] Warren, 214.

publication should be repressed may be
described as those which concern the private life,
habits, acts, and relations of an individual, and
have not legitimate connection with his fitness
for a public office which he seeks or for which
he is suggested.[8]

Although the words of these two jurists sound as fresh
today as they did more than a full century ago, and although
New York state passed the first privacy statute as early as 1903,
it was not until the publication of Dean William L. Prosser's
Handbook of the Law of Torts in 1941 that the modern notion of
privacy began to take shape. Much of what Dean Prosser
proposed in his handbook and later published in a highly
influential article entitled simply "Privacy" was incorporated
first in the second and later the third edition of *Restatement of
the Law: Torts* and also later by the courts into the laws of the
states and the nation. [9]

The right of privacy entered Pennsylvania statutes by the
side door when, in 1953, the commonwealth adopted *The
Uniform Single Publication Act*, which included the following, "
No person shall have more than one cause of action for damages
for libel or slander, or invasion of privacy . . . ." Although the
legislature did not create a right of privacy in this statute, it did
recognize one.[10] The first appellate court decision was rendered
three years later by the Pennsylvania Superior Court, which

---

[8] Warren, 215.

[9] California Law Review, 1960.

[10] 12 Pa.Stat. § 2090.1. Four other statutory sections mention privacy. 18
Pa. Conn. Stat. § 5701 (2002) focuses on wiretapping and electronic
surveillance; 18 Pa. Conn. Stat. § 5703 (2002) focuses on interception,
disclosure and use of wire, electronic and oral communications; 18 Pa. Conn.
Stat. § 7507.1 (2002) makes it a crime to photograph or film without
permission a person who is nude or partially nude; and 42 Pa. Conn. Stat. §
5523 (2002) asserts that a suit for invasion of privacy must be filed within a
year following the invasion.

obviously was uncomfortable with the notion of a right to privacy and so devoted many paragraphs to a discussion of it.[11]

The court reached all the way back to an 1895 act in order to find a statute upon which to base its decision.[12] Since that law stated there was a two-year limitation for injury wrongfully done to the person, the court concluded, "[t]he invasion of privacy is an 'injury wrongfully done to the person' and is therefore controlled by the Act of 1895."[13] Included in this discussion is an attempt to distinguish a privacy tort from libel. "In actions to recover damages for defamation truth is a defense; in action to recover damages for invasion of privacy it is not. Damages in actions of defamation are for an injury to reputation, while damages in action for invasion of privacy are for injury to one's own feelings.[14] Journalists may find some

---

[11] *Hull v. Curtis*, 125 A.2d 644 (Pa. Super. 1956). The first reference to a Pennsylvania right of privacy in the appellate courts was a concurring opinion by Justice Maxey in *Waring v. WDAS Broadcasting Station, Inc.*, 194 A. 631 (Pa. 1937). Three cases in the Common Pleas Courts of Philadelphia County referenced Maxey. In *Harlow v. Buno Co., Inc.*, 36 D. & C. 101 (1939) the right was recognized, but recovery denied under the facts because the invasion was not intentional and was discontinued as soon as the defendant learned its supposed authority to publish a plaintiff's picture was not genuine. In *Clayman v. Bernstein*, 38 D. & C. 543 (1940) the right was again recognized in an action to enjoin the use of a photograph taken by a doctor of a patient without her consent. In *Lisowski v. Jaskiewicz*, 76 D. & C. 79 (1951) the right was again recognized, but preliminary objections were sustained on the ground that the complaint failed to show a violation of the right. Finally, Judge Goodrich said in *Leverton v. Curtis Publishing Co.*, 192 F.2d 974 (3d Cir. 1951), that the publication of a picture by a magazine was an actionable invasion of a plaintiff's right of privacy under the laws of the Commonwealth of Pennsylvania. He added that, since the outlines of the right and the privilege to invade were only dimly marked, the court was required to fashion its decision from the materials at hand without the benefit of an authoritative decision on the exact point involved in Pennsylvania or elsewhere.

[12] 12 Pa. Stat. Ann. § 34 (1895).

[13] Hull, 125 A.2d at 652.

[14] *Hull*, 125 A.2d at 650.

comfort in the court's closing note, "[I]t must not be forgotten that the right of privacy infringes upon freedom of speech and press and clashes with the interest of the public in the free dissemination of news and information, and that these paramount public interests must be considered when placing the necessary limitations upon the right of privacy.[15]

Today, Pennsylvania's laws on privacy differ little from those of the rest of the nation, primarily because this tort is still evolving. The word privacy is not mentioned in the U.S. Constitution, and our American seemingly unquenchable search for technology, exploration, and information is not always compatible with the principles of privacy. Nevertheless, four general forms of privacy are widely recognized: appropriation (often associated with a notion called the right of publicity), intrusion, disclosure, and false light, sometimes called fictionalization. Although the U.S. Supreme Court has ruled fewer than a dozen times on important privacy issues, Pennsylvania Courts have commented on all four forms.

The Pennsylvania Superior Court, in its early examinations of privacy as a legitimate tort, worried about what impact such a right might have upon already established constitutional protections that might conflict with a right to privacy. The court noted, for example, "Without well defined limitations the right of privacy might dangerously encroach upon freedom of speech and freedom of the press. Legal actions for invasion of the right of privacy must not be a vehicle for the establishment of a judicial censorship of the press. The courts are not concerned with establishing canons of good taste for the press or the public.[16] In addition, the court pointed out the limitations of this right when it wrote the following:

> One who is not a recluse must expect comment
> upon his conduct. Likewise, if he submits

---

[15] *Hull*, 125 A.2d at 651.

[16] *Aquino v. Bulletin Company*, 154 A.2d 422, 425 (Pa. Super. 1959).

himself or his work for public approval, as does a candidate for public office, a public official, an actor, an author, or a stunt aviator, he must necessarily pay the price of even unwelcome publicity through reports upon his private life and photographic reproductions of himself and his family, unless these are defamatory or exceed the bounds of fair comment. One who unwillingly comes into the public eye as in the case of a criminal, and even one unjustly charged with crime or the subject of a striking catastrophe, is subject to the limitations on his right to be let alone. Both groups of persons are the objects of legitimate public interest during a period of time after their conduct or misfortune has brought them to the public attention. Publishers are privileged "to satisfy the curiosity of the public as to their leaders, heroes, villains and victims."[17]

It continued, "The liability [in privacy] exists only if the defendant's conduct was such that he should have realized that it would be offensive to persons of ordinary sensibilities. It is only where the intrusion has gone beyond the limits of decency that liability accrues."[18]

Supporting a claim to an invasion of privacy requires demonstrating first a reasonable expectation of privacy. In 1963 the Pennsylvania Supreme Court first addressed the issue of a reasonable expectation of privacy. After an Isobel Forster was involved in an automobile accident with a Francis Martin, Martin's insurance company, the Guardian Mutual Insurance Company, along with the Hays Adjustment Bureau retained

---

[17] *Aquino*, 154 A.2d at 425, 426.
[18] *Aquino*, 154 A.2d at 426.

Michael Manchester, a licensed private detective, to investigation Forster's daily activities in order to ascertain the extent to which she had freedom of movement over her limbs. Manchester conducted the surveillance by assigning a team of two men equipped with motion picture cameras. As a result of being followed, Forster said she became extremely nervous and upset, causing her to have frequent nightmares and hallucinations that required medical treatment.

The court opined that, by making a claim for personal injuries, Forster did not have a reasonable expectation of privacy because she must expect a reasonable inquiry and investigation to be made of her claim. The court also took care to point out that all of the surveillances took place in the open on public thoroughfares where her activities could be observed by passers-by and concluded, "To this extent appellant has exposed herself to public observation and therefore is not entitled to the same degree of privacy that she would enjoy within the confines of her own home."[19] The court also noted that no trespass or spying through windows occurred. From this case, it became clear that persons in public places do not have the same expectation of privacy that they would have in a private location.

Only four years later, the United States Supreme Court weighed in on the issue of an expectation of privacy.[20] Based primarily on FBI recordings from a telephone booth, a gambler was convicted of transmitting wagering information by telephone across state lines. The Court began its analysis by saying the Constitution implies a concern for the right of all persons to a private enclave where they may lead a private life. It noted that, although what persons knowingly expose to the public, even in their own home or office, is not a subject of Fourth Amendment protection, what they seek to preserve as

---

[19] *Forster v Manchester*, 189 A.2d 147, 149 (Pa. 1963).
[20] *Katz v. United States*, 389 U.S. 347 (1967).

private, even in an area accessible to the public (such as a telephone booth), may be constitutionally protected. The Court ruled that the Fourth Amendment governs not only the seizure of tangible items, but extends as well to the recording of oral statements that are overheard even without any trespass. Writes Justice Stewart, "The reach of the [Fourth] amendment cannot turn upon the presence or absence of a physical intrusion into any given enclosure."[21] In essence, the court put forth a rule with a twofold requirement for claiming an invasion of privacy. First, a person have exhibited an actual (subjective) expectation of privacy and, second, that the expectation be one that society is prepared to recognize as reasonable."

In an interesting twist on the expectation of privacy issue, the Pennsylvania Court revisited its earlier pronouncement[22] ruling that, although the law protects the right to keep one's private conversations safe from unauthorized listeners, a basic element of the invasion of privacy tort is the intentional overhearing by someone not intended to be a party to a private conversation. Therefore, even if a conversation is recorded without permission, there is no invasion of privacy if there is no overhearing of the private communication.

After the City of Sharon installed a telephone recording system at its police department headquarters, attorney Marc Lincoln Marks telephoned the department and became aware from an unusual noise on the line that his conversation was being recorded. Although he repeatedly demanded that these recordings be halted, the police department refused.

Marks eventually lost his case because, although his conversations were recorded, he could produce no evidence they were replayed. The tapes were reused every month, and each new use erased the conversations previously recorded. Thus, the tape recording of his conversations were extremely

---

[21] *Katz* 389 U.S. at 353.
[22] *Marks v. Bell Telephone Co. of Pennsylvania*, 331 A.2d. 424 (Pa. 1975).

ephemeral and not be heard by anyone. Writes the court, "Therefore the only ear ever to hear appellant's communication was a mechanical one."[23] It continued, "Because neither the evidence nor the inferences arising therefrom proves that appellant's private conversation were heard by any human ear or that there is some potential they will be heard in the future, the invasion of privacy tort has not been established."

In 1974, the Pennsylvania Supreme Court rendered into law the four types of privacy listed in *Restatement (Second) of Torts* § 652A, "the action for invasion of privacy is actually comprised of [*sic*]four analytically distinct torts: 1) intrusion upon seclusion, 2) appropriation of name or likeness, 3) publicity given to private life, and 4) publicity placing a person in false light."[24] Until then, most of the Pennsylvania decisions dealing with invasions of privacy involved either publicity given to private facts or the appropriation of one's likeness,[25] but in 1975 the court accepted a case in which the invaded interest was the privacy of one's conversations. [26]

---

[23] *Marks*, 331 A.2d at 430.

[24] *Vogel v. W. T. Grant Co.*, 327 A.2d 133, 136 (Pa. 1974).

[25] *Vogel*; *Corabi v Curtis*, 273 A.2d 899 (Pa. 1971); *Bennett v. Norban*, 151 A.2d 476 (Pa. 1959); *Schnabel v. Meredith*, 107 A.2d 860 (Pa. 1954); *Aquino*, and *Hull*.

[26] *Marks v Bell Telephone*, 331 A.2d 424 (Pa. 1975). By this time the legislature had enacted a statute asserting, *inter alia*, "No person shall intercept a communication by telephone or telegraph without permission of the parties to such communication." 18 Pa. Stat. Ann. § 3742 (1974). The court ruled, however, that "Although his conversations were recorded, there is no evidence from which it can be inferred that they were replayed. The record clearly shows and the court found that the tapes were reused every month, each new use erasing the conversations previously recorded on that tape. It would appear the tape recording of appellant's conversations no longer exists and will not be heard by anyone. Therefore the only ear ever to hear appellant's communication was a mechanical one. Because neither the evidence nor the inferences arising therefrom proves that appellant's private conversation were heard by any human ear or that there is some potential

There is today also no Pennsylvania expectation of privacy in a web site.[27] In May 1998, an eighth grade student created a web-site on his home computer and on his own time. Titled "Teacher Sux," the page made derogatory comments about the student's algebra teacher and principal. In order to gain access to the site, a visitor was required to agree to a disclaimer that asserted, among other things, the visitor was not a member of the school district's faculty or administration and that the visitor did not intend to disclose the identity of the web-site creator or intend to cause trouble for that person.

The Commonwealth Court said the disclaimer had no legal effect upon the web-site creator's right to privacy because, among other reasons, the disclaimer does not limit access to the site nor does it inform the viewer of its offensive nature.[28]

"The school district did not violate student's right to privacy when it accessed the web-site," said the court, because the student's web-site was not a protected site, "meaning that only certain viewers could access the site by use of a known password."[29] As such, any user enter the correct search terms could have stumbled upon it. Writes the court, "Once it is posted, the creator loses control of the web-site's destiny and it

---

they will be heard in the future, the invasion of privacy tort has not been established." *Marks*, 331 A.2d at 426.

[27] *J.S. v. Bethlehem Area School District*, 757 A.2d 412 (Pa. Commw. 2000).

[28] In *United States v. Charbonneau*, 979 F. Supp. 1177 (S.D. Ohio 1997), the court ruled that a person did not possess an expectation of privacy for e-mail. The court likened e-mail messages to a letter. A sender reasonably can expect that the contents of a letter remain private only until the time that a recipient receives it. Once received, a sender no longer can control the letter's destiny and, therefore, cannot be granted a reasonable expectation of privacy. Likewise, a creator of a web-site controls a site until the time when it is posted on the Internet. Once posted, a creator loses control of the web-site's destiny, and it may be accessed by anyone on the Internet. Without protecting the web-site, a creator takes the risk of others accessing it once it is posted.

[29] *J.S.*, 757 A.2d at 425.

may be accessed by anyone on the Internet. Without protecting the web-site, the creator takes the risk of other individuals accessing it once it is posted. Accordingly, we conclude that the trial court was correct in its determination that Student maintained no expectation of privacy in the web-site."[30]

Appropriation

Appropriation is often described as a property right; that is, persons own their likeness in much the same way as they own their car. Therefore, several states have passed laws making it illegal to take without permission another person's name or photograph and use it for commercial gain. The right of publicity association with appropriation asserts that persons have a right to control the commercial exploitation of their likeness.

Without doubt the most famous U.S. Supreme Court case on appropriation focused on 15 seconds of a television news broadcast. On the 11 o'clock news of August 30, 1972, the entire 15 second act of Howard Zacchini, a human cannonball performing at the Geauga County Fair in Burton, Ohio, (east of Cleveland) was broadcast by television station WEWS. Zacchini sued, claiming his act was "commercialized" without his consent and the newscast was an "'unlawful appropriation'" of his "'professional property.'"[31]

Although the Supreme Court of Ohio recognized Zacchini's "'right to the publicity value of his performance,'" it ruled against him, saying, "'A TV station has a privilege to report in its newscasts matters of legitimate public interest which would otherwise be protected by an individual's right of publicity, unless the intent was to appropriate the benefit of

---

[30] *J.S.*, 757 A.2d at 425.
[31] *Zacchini* v. *Scripps-Howard Broadcasting Co.* 433 U.S. 562, 564, 565 (1977).

publicity for some non-privileged private use, or unless the actual intent was to injure the individual."[32]

Later, Justice Byron R. White, writing for the U.S. Supreme Court, took care to distinguish appropriation from the three other forms of privacy. While intrusion, disclosure, and false light are based on the idea that private citizens can seek protection from privacy, appropriation is founded upon the assertion that publicity is welcomed, but should be remunerated. White said the problem with broadcasting the entire act is that it "poses a substantial threat to the economic value of that performance."[33] "If the public can see the act free on television," he wrote, "It will be less willing to pay to see it at the fair."[34] The broadcast, White said, constitutes "appropriation of the very activity by which the entertainer acquired his reputation in the first place."[35]

The majority opinion in the first Pennsylvania case to deal with the concept of appropriation did not use the word privacy, but, not surprisingly related the tort to a property right.[36] Fred Waring successfully sued station WDAS because it broadcast, without paying him a fee, an RCA record he had produced with the words "Not licensed for Radio Broadcast." It was Justice George W. Maxey, writing a concurring opinion, who introduced the notion of privacy into Pennsylvania case law, "I think plaintiff's [Waring's] right which was invaded by defendant [station WDAS] was his right to privacy, which is a broader right than a mere right of property."[37] Maxey compared Warning's plight to eavesdropping. He writes, "At common law eavesdropping was considered such an invasion of people's right to privacy that it was treated as something even baser than

---

[32] *Zacchini*, 433 U.S. at 565.
[33] *Zacchini*, 433 U.S. at 575.
[34] *Zacchini*, 433 U.S. at 576.
[35] *Zacchini*, 433 U.S. at 576.
[36] *Waring v. WDIS Broadcasting Station, Inc.,* 194 A. 631 (Pa. 1937).
[37] *Waring, 194 A. 632.*

a civil wrong, to wit, a crime."[38] Broadcasting Warning's record without consent, in essence, Maxey said, makes illegal eavesdroppers out of the audience.

Nevertheless, the Third Circuit Federal Court of Appeals decades later ignored Maxey's idea of eavesdropping, and adopted the majority's notion of a property right concept in privacy and applied it to Albert Ettore, a boxer, who objected to a 1949 television broadcast, without paying him a fee, of his 1936 fight with Joe Louis. Ettore signed a consent form to have the fight filmed, but, since commercial television was not then available, he did not consent to its broadcast. The court extended his property right to television and said the NBC affiliate wrongly appropriated "his livelihood."[39] Although this decision was an early recognition of the mere existence of a right to privacy, most jurists trace the first instance of a Pennsylvania appellate court's establishment of this right to a 1956 state Supreme Court ruling.[40]

An early Pennsylvania case related to appropriation appears an anachronism today.[41] A professional athlete sued because he did not want his name associated with the selling of beer. William Sharman, an all-American basketball player for the Boston Celtics, signed a contract in which he agreed to sell his picture for $125.00. An agency took his picture while he was holding a blowing ball, but the S. Schmidt company, unbeknownst to Sharman, added a beer glass and bottle to his picture when they used it in an advertisement. XXX

After the advertisement appeared, Sharman suffered ridicule and criticism during a few basketball games and, particularly, in Philadelphia, where Schmidt beer is sold. He said the ridicule and criticism caused him concern and worriment. He also said he particularly was concerned over the

---

[38] *Waring, 194 A. 631.*
[39] *Ettore* v. *Philco Television Broadcasting Corp.,* 229 F.2d 485, 490 (1956).
[40] *In theAppeal of Mack*, 126 A.2d 679, 683 (Pa.1956).
[41] *Sharman v Schmidt*, 216 F. Supp. 401 (E.D.Pa. 1963).

possible loss of sports endorsements and over the advertisement's effect on children and parents. In addition, he said he suffered anguish that his contemplated future career as a college coach, his participation in boy's camps activities, and his personal appearances before audiences comprised of parents and children would be threatened. After he sued for an invasion of privacy, Schmidt raised the defense of consent. Sharman had signed a release form stating, in part, that he permits the use of his picture "distorted in character, or form."[42]

The court issued a number of far-reaching comments. First, it asserted, "It cannot be maintained as a principle of law that for an athlete to be associated with an advertisement for beer involves his right to privacy."[43] In addition, the Court said, "Sharman's picture was not substantially altered in content. It remained a bowling picture to which was appended a glass and a bottle of beer."[44] The court's comment that was most damaging to Sharman, however, reaffirmed one of the strongest defenses to any privacy suit: consent. The Court wrote, "One universally accepted principle of the right to privacy is that a consent to an invasion is a complete defense to the appropriation of a plaintiff's likeness to sell products."[45] Finally, the Court pointed out, "A celebrity such as Sharman has a limited right to privacy because of his prominence. His actions and life are subject to a legitimate public curiosity."[46] It concluded, "The ... picture ... did not violate the plaintiff's [Sharman's] 'right of publicity.'"[47]

The court's ruling would appear to hold some significance for using computers to alter digital photographs. As long as the photograph is not "substantially altered in

---

[42] *Sharman*, 216 F. Supp at 401.

[43] *Sharman*, 216 F.Supp. at 405.

[44] *Sharman*, 216 F.Supp. at 406.

[45] *Sharman*, 216 F.Supp. at 406, 7.

[46] *Sharman*, 216 F.Supp. at 407.

[47] *Sharman*, 216 F.Supp. at 408.

content," the court seems to be asserting, then changes are not illegal. Journalists would also be well advised, as a result of this opinion, to seek consent when the question of appropriation comes up.

This ruling, the court said, also was consistent with a Fifth Circuit court ruling in a similar case. Pabst Beer, had used a picture of All-American Quarterback, Davie O'Brien (who subsequently became a star for the Philadelphia Eagles) on a calendar which contained advertisements for its beer. Although O'Brien had never signed a written release and had not been paid for the use of his picture, a district court ruled there had been implied consent. The Fifth Circuit sustaining the dismissal and accepted the reasoning of the lower court in reference to the use of an athlete's picture in connection with an advertisement for beer, writing, "[t]he business of making and selling beer is a legitimate and eminently respectable business and people of all walks and views in life, without injury to or reflection upon themselves, drink it, and that any association of O'Brien's picture with a glass of beer could not possibly disgrace or reflect upon or cause him damage."[48] Therefore, the Third Circuit wrote, "We hold that the use of his picture in the advertisement . . . was [not] an intrusion upon his rights which is outrageous or beyond the limits of common decency, and therefore is not an invasion which warrants relief by this Court."[49] In short, the court said that the release Sharman signed for Studio Associates, Inc., for Ted Bates & Company, and for their nominees (i.e., here Schmidt) was a valid and binding contract releasing them from any liability for a reasonable and lawful use of the pictures.

---

[48] *Sharman*, 216 F.Supp. at 405. See also *O'Brien v. Pabst Sales Co.*, 124 F.2d 167 (5th Cir. 1941).

[49] *Sharman*, 216 F.Supp. at 407.

Disclosure

Disclosure is what Warren and Brandeis had in mind when they wrote their *Harvard Law Review* article on privacy. Disclosure was to them and remains today, at least in large part, a euphemism for gossip. Giving highly offensive publicity about private matters not of concern to the public constitutes disclosure. This form of privacy is often referred to as the right to be let alone. Pennsylvanian Carl F. Schnabel sued using this theory when Charles M. Meredith, publisher of the Quakertown *Free Press,* ran a front page story January 24, 1952, in which it was noted that the state police six months earlier had "seized seven slot machines after a raid on the estate of Carl Schnabel."[50] Unimpressed, the Pennsylvania Supreme Court ruled, "By his possession of the slot machines, the appellant [Schnabel] relinquished his right to be let alone."[51] The court said, "In publishing a fact already known to the public . . . publisher cannot be said to have exceeded the limits of decency."[52]

The limits of decency are difficult to recognize, however, and a mere two years later this sweeping approach to disclosure was reevaluated. According the Pennsylvania Superior Court, Theresa Aquino, against her parent's wishes, secretly married John N. Masciocchi before a Justice of the Peace after he promised to provide a home for her and later marry her again in a church. When she pressed him to keep his promises, "He told her that he did not intend to keep them, and that he married her only to spite her parents who had been opposed to his courting her."[53] Theresa, not surprisingly, immediately sued for divorce. Although her suit and the resulting divorce decree were published by the Philadelphia newspapers, her parents, quite surprisingly, managed to keep

---

[50] *Schnabel v. Meredith,* 107 A.2d 860, 861 (Pa. 1954).
[51] *Schnabel,* 107 A.2d at 863.
[52] *Schnabel,* 107 A.2d at 863.
[53] *Aquino,* 154 A.2d at 426.

both her marriage and divorce a secret from their friends and relatives. Of the events so far, the Court asserted the following as it relates to disclosure of highly offense private information.

> Theresa's marriage and her divorce were newsworthy events. Newspapers had a right to publish such information. They also had a right to quote from or republish the opinion filed by the court. Publishing these events which were included in public records does not constitute an unwarranted invasion of the right of privacy of the parties involved, or as a general rule, not even of other persons named in the records, providing the facts have not ceased to be newsworthy through the lapse of time.[54]

The *Sunday Bulletin,* however, was not content to let alone this strange turn of events. On December 3, 1950, in the *American Weekly,* a *Bulletin* supplement, appeared a story the court said was "bedecked with an 'illustrated' drawing covering over half of the page," was "not written in the style of a news article," and contained an "embellished and fictionalized" account under the title "'Marriage for Spite.'"[55] The court asserted, "The figures pictured bore no resemblance to Theresa and John whom they illustrated" and "the Bulletin article, read as a whole . . . [presented] a sensational version of facts embellished with matter drawn from the author's imagination."[56]

Recognizing that defining "highly offensive" is not easy, the Court refused to state that, as a matter of law, the article constituted an illegal disclosure. It also refused, though, to overrule the jury's judgment that, as a matter of fact, it was an invasion of privacy. The Court explained its position this way:

---

[54] *Aquino,* 154 A.2d at 427.
[55] *Aquino,* 154 A.2d at 427.
[56] *Aquino,* 154 A.2d at 429.

The publication of a newsworthy event should always be privileged, unless its presentation is such that the intrusion upon the lives of the parties named in it *clearly* [emphasis in the original] goes beyond the limits of decency. That these limits cannot be precisely defined, however, is no justification for reversing the jury's findings in a case like this one. The evidence establishes that the plaintiff's [Theresa's parents] annoyance came almost entirely from the revelation of the fact, not theretofore known to their friends and relatives, that Theresa had been married and divorced. The action is a personal action and the defendant [*Sunday Bulletin*] is not liable to the appelles [Michael and Nancy Aquino] for what it related about Theresa, but only for what it related about them.[57]

Although this case does not fall exclusively within the disclosure category, having elements of false light, it is an excellent example of how the court approached this subject before Dean Prosser's famous 1960 article on privacy. It also serves as a warning to journalists that what constitutes highly offense private information is defined ultimately by a judge or jury.

The four essential elements of disclosure are explained at length in a case can be traced to a newspaper article, based information supplied by the Department of Public Welfare, that revealed facts concerning the private lives of an applicant for public welfare benefits and her family. The Department altered some of the facts about a Brigitte Harris in order to disguise her identity and fashioned a fictionalized account of the difficulties

---

[57] *Aquino*, 154 A.2d at 430.

she had when applying for benefits. The account was sent to various newspapers in northeast Pennsylvania for inclusion as part of a regular public service column. The purpose of the column was to increase the public understanding of the department's operations, policies, and available services.

The court said the first element of a claim that publicity was given to private facts is that publicity must exist. Interestingly enough, the mere fact that the article appeared in a newspaper, said the court, is insufficient by itself to establish publicity. In addition, the disclosed facts necessarily must identify a particular person. If no readers recognize the exposed person, then there is no communication and so no publicity. Harris said that, from the information in the column, at least 17 persons told her they immediately recognized her as the purportedly fictional character in the account. The court said 17 is enough to assert that the information is now a matter of public knowledge.

The second element requires that the publicity involve a private fact. A private fact is one that has not already been made public. Thus, readers of a newspaper must not have prior knowledge of the publicized private fact: there can be no liability when the publicity reveals facts readers already know. The court rejected the newspaper's claim that the facts already were known simply because the column was distributed by the welfare department.

The third element requires that a reasonable person of ordinary sensibilities would find such publicity highly offensive. The publicity must be more than simply unwanted or unwelcomed facts. In making this determination, the customs of the time and place, the occupation of Harris, and the habits of her neighbors and fellow citizens are germane. The private facts must be made public in such a manner so as to outrage or cause mental suffering, shame, or humiliation to a person of ordinary sensibilities. Here, the court said this element finds support from both the privacy protection given welfare applicants by the public welfare code and from a commonsense analysis of the information.

The final element, a defense often available to the media, exempts from liability those facts which are of legitimate concern to the public, such as official court records open to public inspection. The court noted that the right of privacy competes with the freedom of the press and with the interest of the public in the free dissemination of news and information; these public interests, it asserted, must be considered when placing the necessary limitations upon the right of privacy.

Nevertheless, there is no legitimate public concern, said the court, in giving publicity to the actual circumstances of a person's application for assistance where intimate personal facts are revealed in such a way as to imply that those facts are true and where the personal facts are unnecessary to aid those interested in receiving advice in their applications for assistance. None of this information was necessary to understand or respond to the letter's request for aid printed in the advice column. Therefore, there was no legitimate public concern in giving publicity to the intimate personal facts set forth in the article.

Nor can a newspaper take solace because it did not solicit the information.. Writes the court, "There is no exception to the tort of invasion of privacy for giving publicity to the private life of another where the party giving such publicity does so on the basis of an unsolicited receipt of the private information. Applicants for welfare benefits would be justifiably appalled at having the confidential and highly personal information they provide publicized in a newspaper."[58]

The fourth element--facts of legitimate concern to the public--was used successfully to defend a newspaper in another

---

[58] *Harris*, 483 A.2d at 1388.

case, however.[59] After William R. Culver and Carole A. Culver were informed by school administrators of the Port Allegany School District that the district intended to request that their son, Wayne, repeat the third grade, the Culvers sought a second opinion from a certified school psychologist. They then requested reimbursement for the cost of the evaluation, $225.75, and the request was presented by Superintendent of Schools Ronald Ungerer to the members of the school board at a public meeting.

A reporter from the Port Allegany Reporter Argus wrote two articles about the reimbursement request. They both revealed that Wayne had been diagnosed with a learning disability, information that had been disclosed and was discussed openly during the public meeting of the school board. The Culvers claimed that the published information constituted an invasion of their right to privacy because it was personal and private information they did not wish to have disseminated to the general public.

The court said, though, that the fact the school district was being asked to pay with tax dollars the cost of a privately retained psychologist who had examined a pupil was newsworthy. Therefore, so long as the facts were reported accurately and truthfully, the newspaper cannot be held liable for invasion of privacy by reporting facts revealed in a public meeting.

A federal court also ruled that this fourth element--facts of legitimate concern to the public--protected a newspaper from an invasion of privacy suit.[60] In this case, Diane Morgan Chambon said she was promised by reporter Mark Calender, in the hallway of the Court of Common Pleas of Allegheny County, Pennsylvania, and elsewhere, that her conversations with him were off the record and that they would not be used in

---

[59] *Culver v. Port Allegany Reporter Argus*, 598 A.2d 54 (Pa. Super. 1991).

[60] *Morgan v. Celender*, 780 F. Supp. 307 (W.D. Pa. 1992)

a page one, October 28, 1988, *Valley News* article about her daughter and her former husband Charles Morgan, at one time chief of the New Bethlehem Police Department, who had been charged with abusing Heather. Diane Chambon also said she was told that a photograph of her and her daughter Heather would be a silhouette and that no names would be used. In fact, the names were provided with a picture, along with the caption, "Heather Morgan, a victim of sexual abuse, talks with her mother, Diane."[61]

The Western Pennsylvania district court said that the prosecution of a former police chief charged with heinous crimes against a minor clearly is newsworthy as is sexual abuse of minor children. It also pointed out that the name and age of the victim and the position of the accused were not private facts, but were elements of the offense. Since these facts were part of the public record in state court, they clearly were within the public domain. Significantly, the court writes, "[t]he news media has the right to publish such items, even if a reporter promises that such additional facts, not of record, would be 'off the record.' The law provides that anyone who desires to discuss matters of public concern with a reporter does so at his or her peril that the matter may be published."[62] It added an important note, "It matters not, in our judgment, that the information and photograph may have been obtained illegally, unethically or deceptively by the reporter."[63] Since publication of these facts, said the court, is protected by the First Amendment, a damage award on such matters of legitimate public concern would be an impermissible burden under the First Amendment.

It is apparent that attacks on the legitimate public concern prong of an invasion of privacy case are not uncommon, but rarely successful. An ingenious one was

---

[61] *Morgan*, 789 F.Supp at 308.
[62] *Morgan*, 789 F.Supp at 310.
[63] *Morgan*, 789 F.Supp at 310.

proffered by William Lee, the owner and operator of Denver Nursing Home, who participated in Pennsylvania's federally funded Medical Assistance Program.[64] In January 1982, the Pennsylvania Attorney General's office brought against Lee and others criminal charges questioning the propriety of cost reports filed by the nursing home with the Pennsylvania Department of Public Welfare. The charges were dismissed in December on the grounds that they were filed after statute of limitations had run out. Robert Gentzel, Pennsylvania Attorney General's assistant press secretary, told a reporter that the United States Attorney for the Eastern District of Pennsylvania had asked for the state's records. As a result of that conversation, a newspaper article was published saying that the Justice Department was considering filing its own charges against Lee, who, subsequently, sued, asserting that the news story violated his state and federal rights to privacy.

Lee maintained, among other things, that the investigation was not of public concern primarily because grand jury proceedings and other pre-indictment investigations traditionally are enshrouded in secrecy. The court observed, however, that post-indictment records generally are open to the public and there is no statute prohibiting disclosure of pre-indictment information to the media. It pointed out that law enforcement officials sometimes reveal many details about their investigations to reporters. Gentzel's truthful revelation, therefore, was not an unusual practice that would justify supporting a claim to invasion of privacy. Moreover, said the court, the subject of the investigation--a nursing home allegedly misusing public funds--surely is of legitimate public concern. Thus, the court rejected on state law a claim of invasion of privacy.

Lee's federal claim, though, is much more convoluted. In effect, he said that the United States Supreme Court's

---

[64] *Lee v. Mihalich*, 630 F. Supp. 152 (E.D. Pa. 1986).

rejection of a Kentucky privacy claim provides a basis for supporting a claim in Pennsylvania.[65] Lee said the Kentucky claim was rejected only because, unlike Pennsylvania, the Kentucky constitution does not recognize reputation as a liberty or property interest. The court responded that the greater right to privacy granted by the Pennsylvania constitution still does not provide a state law basis for a federal claim and so also dismissed Lee's federal suit for invasion of privacy.

Marie M. Faison was not less ingenious in her argument for objecting to the disclosure of what she considered private information.[66] Faison said the following five statements in her presentence report violate her federal, state, and common law right to privacy: (1) she was diagnosed as having cervical cancer; (2) she tested positive for syphilis; (3) she tested positive for the HIV virus; (4) she was diagnosed as having a severe character disorder--schizoid personality severe with strong paranoid trends; and (5) she threatened the life of a caseworker while in court concerning the foster care and custody of one of her children.

The district court approached Faison's argument by noting first that the United States Supreme Court recognizes a constitutionally protected privacy interest in two areas: (1) an individual interest in avoiding disclosure of personal matters and (2) an interest in independence in making certain kinds of important decisions.[67] It then noted that the third circuit has held that medical records are protected from disclosure by the first interest, the confidentiality branch of the right to privacy.[68] It also held, though, that governmental intrusion into private medical records is permitted if, after balancing the interests of the individual with those of society, the court determines that

---

[65] *Paul v. Davis*, 424 U.S. 693 (1976).

[66] *Faison v. Parker*, 823 F. Supp. 1198 (E.D. Pa. 1993).

[67] *Whalen v. Roe*, 429 U.S. 589 (1977)

[68] *United States v. Westinghouse Elec. Corp.*, 638 F.2d 570, 577 (3d Cir. 1980).

societal interest in disclosure outweighs the individual's interest in privacy.

This balancing by the court, however, is extensive. It said seven factors must be considered when deciding whether an intrusion into an individual's privacy is justified: (1) the type of record requested; (2) the information it does or might contain; (3) the potential for harm in any subsequent nonconsensual disclosure; (4) the injury from disclosure to the relationship in which the record was generated; (5) the adequacy of the safeguards to prevent unauthorized disclosure; (6) the degree of need for access; and (7) whether there is an express statutory mandate, articulated public policy, or other recognized public interest militating toward access.[69]

Focusing on the last three factors as they related to a presentence report, the court concluded that, since there is strong public interest in having the court gain access to these records, there is a high degree of need for the court to gain access to them, and the state safeguards against unauthorized disclosure are strong, Ms. Faison's constitutional right to privacy in the nondisclosure of her medical and mental health records was not violated. It noted, for example, that this information guides the sentencing court in determining an appropriate facility in which to incarcerate Ms. Faison, and enables the prison system to provide Ms. Faison with necessary medical and psychiatric attention.[70] Strong protection against disclosure can be found in Pennsylvania statutes and in the Pennsylvania Rule of Criminal Procedure. The fact that this information is maintained in court, probation, prison, and attorney files, and may not be in locked cabinets, does not render the safeguards inadequate.[71] The court said the same balancing test produces the same result for Pennsylvania.

---

[69] *Westinghouse*, 638 F.2d at 578.

[70] *Faison*, 823 F. Supp. at 1201.

[71] *Faison*, 823 F. Supp. at 1204.

The court's discussion of Mrs. Faison's disclosure violations asserted in her common law theory may be of some interest to journalists. She said that unconstitutional disclosure has occurred because the presentence report is contained in numerous files, and was typed in a typing pool. She said that simply marking the records confidential and having a statute requiring the records not be open to the public is inconclusive evidence that the report does not meet the publicity requirement. The court, however, rejected her arguments, saying there was no disclosure to the general public, only to those persons who had a need to know.

In yet another case focusing in large part on matters of legitimate public concern, the Pennsylvania Superior Court also ruled against a police officer.[72] In 1987, Michael Santillo, a former police officer, ran for district justice in Montgomery County. Prior to the election, a young woman told the press that, eight years before, when she was sixteen years old, he made unwanted sexual advances toward her. A resulting news story revealed that the girl's mother, Sandra Adams, had filed a formal complaint to the police department and sought to press charges against Santillo. Although her daughter was given a polygraph test that indicated that she was telling the truth, the mother signed a release stating that she would not press criminal charges nor bring a civil action against Santillo if he resigned from the police force. A week later Santillo resigned and later brought suit for invasion of privacy against newspapers, the reporters, Adams, and her daughter, and two police officers who released the information about the polygraph test .

Santillo met one element of an invasion of privacy suit when the Pennsylvania Superior Court said that this information could cause a reasonable person of ordinary sensibilities to be offended. Allegations of sexual abuse of a minor, it noted, are

---

[72] *Santillo v. Reedel*, 634 A.2d 264 (Pa. Super. 1993).

of a type that certainly could cause shame or humiliation. Offensiveness notwithstanding, the court also pointed out the information was of legitimate concern to the public. Santillo was running for public office; he was seeking a position that would enable him to judge the conduct of others and to determine whether their conduct was in conformity with the law. Therefore, a claim that he violated the law was relevant and newsworthy even if the substance of the complaint was false. This newsworthiness successfully defended against his claim of publicity given to private facts.

Without question, the topic that has produced the most interest, and perhaps the most lawsuits, in the area of disclosure is rape. This topic may self-destruct, however, by its continuing exposure. If rape continues to occupy increasingly the attention of the news media, then it may lose whatever offensive connotations are left. When rape victims willingly participate in interviews with journalists, these victims, by their very participation, demonstrate that revealing the existence of a rape is no longer highly offensive to the average private person.

The first disclosure privacy case involving rape to come before the U.S. Supreme Court stemmed from a Georgia television station's broadcasting the name of 17-year-old rape victim, Cynthia Cohn. Her father, Martin, sued, charging "his right to privacy had been invaded by the television broadcast giving the name of his deceased daughter."[73] Cohn relied in part on a section of the Georgia Code "which makes it a misdemeanor to publish or broadcast the name or identity of a rape victim."[74] The television station said the First and Fourteenth Amendments gave it a privilege to use the name. When the case found its way to the United States Supreme Court, Justice Byron R. White defined the disclosure form of privacy as "a zone of privacy surrounding every individual, a

---

[73] *Cox Broadcasting Corp. v. Cohn,* 420 U.S. 469, 474 (1975).
[74] *Cox,* 420 U.S. at 472.

zone within which the State may protect him from intrusion by the press."[75] The media may invade legally that zone, however, if they have adequate justification. The justification put forth by station WSB relied on the fact that the name of the victim was obtained by reporter Thomas Wassell when examining the rapist's indictments made available for public inspection in the courtroom.

White accepted the station's argument, saying names obtained from public court records do justify disclosure of offensive private information. He reasoned that, since in our society citizens have "limited time and resources with which to observe at first hand the operations of . . . government," they rely "necessarily upon the press" to inform them of these operations.[76] Indeed, White asserts that the media have a "great responsibility . . . to report fully and accurately the proceedings of government, and official records and documents open to the public are the basic data of governmental operations."[77] In particular, reporting of "judicial proceedings . . . serve[s] to guarantee the fairness of trials and to bring to bear the beneficial effects of public scrutiny upon the administration of justice."[78] White added, "The developing law surrounding the tort of invasion of privacy recognizes a privilege in the press to report the events of judicial proceedings."[79]

White gave two more reasons that are still accepted today. One is "that the interests of privacy fade when the information involved already appears on the public record."[80] He wrote, "The freedom of the press to publish that information [from public records] appears to us to be of critical importance to our type of government in which the citizenry is the final judge of

---

[75] Cox, 420 U.S. at 487.
[76] Cox, 420 U.S. at 491.
[77] Cox, 420 U.S. at 492.
[78] Cox, 420 U.S. at 492.
[79] Cox, 420 U.S. at 493.
[80] Cox, 420 U.S. at 494.

the proper conduct of public business."[81] Another reason is that the Court expressed a reluctance "to embark on a course that would make public records generally available to the media but forbid their publication if offensive to the sensibilities of the supposed reasonable man."[82] The problem with such a course of action, according to White, is this: "The rule would invite timidity and self-censorship and very likely lead to the suppression of many items that would otherwise be published and that should be made available to the public."[83] The states can protect privacy interests, he asserted, "by means which avoid public documentation or other exposure of private information."[84] This case firmly established the principle that accurate reports of judicial proceedings are privileged from privacy suits.

In spite of this decision, Florida in 1983 still had on the books a statute that made it illegal to "'print, publish, or broadcast in any instrument of mass communication' the name of the victim of a sexual offense."[85] The United States Supreme Court addressed this law by asking the question whether a state statute violates the First and Fourteenth Amendments if it imposes strict liability for invasion of privacy when a newspaper publishes truthful information legally obtained from records of a state agency.[86] More specifically, does a law violate the Constitution if it asserts that a newspaper automatically is guilty of negligence when it publishes the private fact of a rape victim's name obtained from government records?

There was no hint that false light was also involved because Jacqueline Lotson, an intern at the *Florida Star,* copied

---

[81] *Cox,* 420 U.S. at 495.
[82] *Cox,* 420 U.S. at 495.
[83] *Cox,* 420 U.S. at 496.
[84] Cox, 420 U.S. at 496.
[85] FS § 794.03 (1987).
[86] *Florida Star v. B.J.F.* 491 U.S. 524 (1989).

the police report verbatim, including the victim's full name, on a blank duplicate of the Department's form. In her complaint, the victim asserted that the news story was published intentionally and with reckless indifference towards her and her well being. She also said that, as a result of the article, she was caused to suffer shame and humiliation, and emotional pain and suffering. Although she sought only $18,000 in damages (a dollar for each subscriber), the jury awarded her $75,000 in compensatory damages and $25,000 in punitive damages, feeling the newspaper did in fact act with reckless indifference to the rights of others. The Court overruled the award, saying that finding a newspaper "civilly liable for publishing the name of a rape victim which it had obtained from a publicly released police report" violates the First Amendment.[87]

It is important to note that the Court did not hold that a state may never punish a newspaper for publishing the name of a rape victim. As is often the case, the Court preferred a much more narrow ruling. It held only that, if a newspaper publishes truthful information lawfully obtained, the government may constitutionally impose punishment, if at all, only when a statute is narrowly designed to support a public interest of the highest order. Preventing the press from publishing a rape victim's name obtained from the police does not constitute a state interest of the highest order.

The single Pennsylvania privacy case related to rape also deals with public records, but appears to have only a little relevancy to the media. The Commonwealth Court ruled constitutional a Pennsylvania statute requiring victims of rape and incest to report the incidents to a law enforcement or child protection agency before becoming eligible to receive a state subsidy for an abortion.[88] Of some interest to journalists are the

---

[87] *Florida Star,* 526.

[88] *Fisher v Dept. of Public Welfare,* 543 A.2d 177 (Pa. Commw. 1988). Statute is 18 Pa. Conn. Stat. § 3201-3220.

court's assertions that "protection from disclosure is not absolute" and that "the court must balance the individual's privacy right against the countervailing public interest."[89]

The appellate court considered at length the testimony of Dr. Ellen Frank, an expert on the subject of the psychological consequences of rape victimization, testimony directly relevant to journalists who report police news. According to the court, Dr. Frank presented two major reasons for not revealing identities of rape victims, "First and most important, fear of retaliation by the assailant; and second, post-traumatic depression and anxiety."[90]

The court then took note that "Dr. Frank acknowledged that the fear of retaliation is largely unfounded."[91] "Additionally," the court stated, "A victim's and the public's perception of the police treatment of a rape victim is not consistent with the professionalism found in large police departments today. *It is the media, Dr. Frank acknowledged, which continues to misportray the investigation of rape reports and treatment of victims* (emphasis added)."[92]

The court appears to be suggesting that the highly offensive connotations often associated with being a rape victim have been ameliorated to a large degree. Secondly, the court once more affirmed the defense of newsworthiness, giving more credence to the importance of public interest as a justification for invasion of privacy. The third and perhaps most important aspect of this case to journalists is the assertion that investigations of rape and the treatment of rape victims have been not been covered well by the media. Perhaps the media have become victims of their own errors. More sensitive and accurate reporting of rape may very well contribute to more

---

[89] Fisher, 543 A.2d at 179.
[90] Fisher, 543 A.2d at 179.
[91] Fisher, 543 A.2d at 180.
[92] Fisher, 543 A.2d at 181.

widespread acceptance by the courts and the public of public disclosure of the names of victims of rape.

False Light or Fictionalization
The *Aquino* court used the term "fictionized" in an attempt to characterize the form of privacy at issue there. Later, the term fictionalization would come to be associated with the false light form of privacy, one that has received considerable attention from the courts. Put simply, false light or fictionalization results from communication of nondefamatory false information. While often confusingly similar to libel, false light can be distinguished because the information communicated is not defamatory, but only highly offensive to a reasonable person.

The first false light case to come before the United States Supreme Court originated in Pennsylvania. The facts of this case are extremely complex in part because it took a quarter of a century from the original event for this law suit to reach the high Court.

For 19 hours on September 11 and 12, 1952, James Hill, his wife, son, and daughter were held hostage in their own sunburn Philadelphia home at Whitemarsh by three escaped convicts. After being released unharmed, they expressly noted that the convicts treated them "courteously, had not molested them, and had not been violent."[93] Joseph Hayes published a novel, called *The Desperate Hours,* about their ordeal, which was made into a Broadway play, reviewed by *Life* magazine. The pictures accompanying the review showed the son being "'roughed up'" by a convict and the "daughter biting the hand of a convict to make him drop a gun."[94] Hill sued, charging "the Life article was intended to, and did, give the impression that

---

[93] *Time* v. *Hill*, 385 U.S. 374, 378 (1967).
[94] *Time* v. *Hill*, 385 U.S. at 377.

the play mirrored the Hill family's experience, which to the knowledge of the defendant [Life]' . . . was false and untrue."'[95]

Writing for the Court, Justice William J. Brennan, makes reference to an earlier New York State case involving hall-of-fame baseball picture Warren Spahn, who objected to an unauthorized biography that the trial court said gave an "inaccurate and distorted" view of his "personal and private life."[96]   The appeals court asserted that Spahn owned his "personality," which could not be "fictionalized" and "exploited for . . . commercial benefit through the medium of an unauthorized biography."[97]   Brennan applied the appellate court's notion of fictionalization to Hill, but added that, in order to win a privacy case, Hill would have to show that the fictionalization was done with actual malice, that is with knowledge that the story was false or with reckless disregard of the truth. This case achieved significance and is still the law in Pennsylvania because, even though the state is thought by the Court to have a greater duty to protect private citizens than it does to protect public officials, private persons must show the high fault of actual malice to win damages in a privacy case for the simple reason that invasion of privacy is a lesser injury than is libel.

The only other false light case to come before the U.S. Supreme Court originated only a few miles from the western Pennsylvania border. When the Silver Bridge across the Ohio River at Point Pleasant, West Virginia, collapsed in 1976, killing Melvin Cantrell and 43 other persons, Joseph Eszterhas, a reporter at the Cleveland *Plain Dealer,* owned by Forest City Publishing Company, was assigned to cover the story. Five months later Eszterhas wrote a follow-up story even though Melvin's widow, Margaret, was not home at any time during his

---

[95] *Time v. Hill,* 385 U.S. at 378.
[96] *Time v.Hill,* 385 U.S. at 386.
[97] *Time v .Hill,* 385 U.S. at 386.

visit. The story "stressed the family's abject poverty," noting the "dirty and dilapidated conditions of the Cantrell home," and carried comments by Cantrell saying she refused offers of money from townspeople.[98]

Cantrell sued on the basis of the false light theory of privacy, charging that Eszterhas' story was false and made her and her family "objects of pity and ridicule," "causing them to suffer outrage, mental distress, shame, and humiliation."[99] Justice Potter Stewart, writing for the Court, described the follow-up feature as "calculated falsehood" in large part because Eszterhas falsely "implied that Mrs. Cantrell had been present during his visit to her home."[100] In an important footnote, Stewart points out that the court of appeals correctly found there was "insufficient evidence to support the jury's verdict against the photographer" because the photographs "were fair and accurate depictions of the people and scenes he found at the Cantrell residence."[101] This case is highly significant because the Court found that reporters who write a story saying they talked with someone not present at an interview are guilty of a "calculated falsehood" and so of actual malice. Such an action constitutes knowingly publishing a falsehood and is, consequently, sufficient fault to be convicted of an invasion of privacy.

Years before the U.S. Supreme Court instituted the requirement of showing actual malice in order to win a false light privacy case, a Pennsylvania case focused on this same issue. Eleanor Sue Leverton, when only ten years old, was hit by a car in 1947 in Birmingham, Alabama. A journalist photographed a woman bystander lifting Leverton to her feet. Nearly two years later, the Curtis Publishing Company of

---

[98] *Cantrell v. Forest City Pub. Co., 419 U S.* 245, 248 (1974).

[99] *Cantrell*, 419 U S. at 248.

[100] *Cantrell*, 419 U S. at 253.

[101] *Cantrell*, 419 U S. at 253.

Pennsylvania purchased the photograph and printed it in an article focusing on pedestrian carelessness.

This is such an early privacy case that the court takes care to note that Curtis admits the existence of the right to privacy in Pennsylvania.[102] It also pointed out that Leverton admits, in turn, the publication of her photograph the day after the accident by a Birmingham newspaper did not invade her privacy.[103] Therefore, the court focused on two questions. Did the 20-month lapse between the accident and the publication of the photograph take away the justification of newsworthiness? The court reveals by this question that, even at an early stage in the development of the privacy tort, newsworthiness is a defense to an invasion of privacy suit. Although the court did not tackle the difficult question of how much time must pass before the defense of newsworthiness is completely vitiated, it did rule, "The immunity from liability for the original publication was not lost through lapse of time when the same picture was again published."[104]

The second question asks whether the newsworthiness privilege was lost "by the using of the plaintiff's [Leverton's] picture, not in connection with a news story, but as an illustration heading an article on pedestrian traffic accidents?"[105] Answering its own question, the court asserts, "This particular publication was an actionable invasion of [the] . . . right of privacy" because "the use of her picture had nothing at all to do with her accident."[106] This case is important to the false light form of privacy, though, because the court also ruled that the photograph falsely indicated the little girl was

---

[102] *Leverton v. Curtis Publishing Company,* 192 F.2d. 974, 975 (1951).

[103] *Leverton,* 192 F.2d. at 976.

[104] *Leverton,* 192 F.2d. at 977.

[105] *Leverton,* 192 F.2d. at 976.

[106] *Leverton,* 192 F.2d. at 977.

negligent, when, in fact, it was the driver of the automobile who was careless.[107]

A not unimportant collateral issue in the Leverton case is the court's rulings on appropriation. That appropriation and false light could be considered in the same case shows how closely the four forms of privacy are related to each other. Leverton argued that Curtis made "commercial use" of the photograph and so illegally appropriated her image. The court, however, ruled that all publication of photographs in newspapers and magazines are used commercially. Such publications, though, do not constitute "an appropriation for a commercial use."[108]

Another example of false light is a case brought by a disgruntled Pennsylvania hunter against CBS, which broadcast a nationwide, one-and-a-half hour, prime-time program called "The Guns of Autumn." The section objected to, however, lasted only a few seconds and comprised only three short scenes. The first scene shows geese walking; the second shows hunters arising from a blind of cornstalks and shooting in a horizontal direction; the third shows hunters walking in a cleared cornfield picking up dead geese. Claire Randy Uhl sued, claiming these approximately 60 seconds of videotape portrayed him in a false light because the editing of this sequence of events wrongly made it appear that he and his fellow Nimrods shot geese who were on the ground.

Even if Uhl was portrayed by CBS in a false light, the first problem faced by the court was determining whether or not such a portrayal would be highly offensive to a reasonable person. The federal appeals court noted in this regard, "It appears from the testimony at trial that in wide reaches of America west of the Hudson where the flights of wild geese darken the noonday sky this is a rather nasty thing to say about

---

[107] *Leverton*, 192 F.2d. at 978.
[108] *Leverton*, 192 F.2d. at 977.

a hunter."[109] Thus, the court said there was enough evidence to allow a jury to decide what would be the reaction of a reasonable person.

Next, the court addresses a rather complex legal issue that demonstrates the subtle similarities and differences between libel and privacy. In *Time* v. *Hill,* a privacy case, the U.S. Supreme Court ruled that, in order for private persons to win a privacy case, they must meet the same high standard of actual malice that public officials must meet to win a libel case. Thus, in order for private persons to win a false light privacy case, they must show that the persons who invaded their privacy either knew the information was false when they communicated it or recklessly disregarded the truth. Twelve years after *Time* v. *Hill*, in *Herbert v. Lando,* a libel case, the high Court said a libel plaintiff is required to show subjective state of mind in order to prove that a person accused of libel is guilty of the fault of actual malice. Commonsense also seems to suggest that the only way to prove a person held a reckless disregard for the truth is to look at what was the person's subjective attitude toward the truth when that person communicated a false statement.

The CBS attorneys asserted strongly that the subjective state of mind requirement to show actual malice in libel should also be applied to show actual malice in privacy. The court disagreed, however, and said that, *since Gertz v. Welch* allowed states to set their own standard of fault,[110] it was not going to apply the state of mind requirement to show actual malice in a libel case to the actual malice standard in a privacy case.

An ironic twist appears in this rather complex decision. When Lando wanted to prove CBS guilty of actual malice, he requested outtakes from the 60 Minutes broadcast that he felt

---

[109] *Uhl v. Columbia Broadcasting Systems,* Inc., 476 F.Supp. 1134 (W.D.Pa. 1979).

[110] *Gertz v. Welch,* 418 U.S. 323 (1979).

libeled him. Outtakes are videotape or film clips that are not used in the actual broadcast. Lando felt that, if he could find an outtake supporting his position, then he would have proof that CBS knew the 60 Minutes broadcast was false when it was aired, thus meeting one of the requirements for showing actual malice. To prevent Lando from gaining access to the outtakes, CBS proposed an editorial privilege, saying the First Amendment protected a television network from revealing the editorial process. The high Court, however, rejected the idea of an editorial process and ordered CBS to give the outtakes to Lando. Ironically, because Uhl did not ask for the outtakes, CBS reversed its earlier position and asserts now that Uhl could not show actual malice precisely because he did not request the outtakes. In a scathing comment, the federal appellate court rejected the CBS position:

> The implication of this argument to the court was that a poor man or even a man of some means has no business bringing litigation in court unless he can afford the services of a large double-breasted law firm with platoons of young credit card-carrying associates who can fan out all over the country on a search-and-depose mission. To suggest that they cannot have their day in court without the orgy of discovery that now attends most lawsuits in Federal Court between well-heeled corporate litigants is indeed a bleak prospect for American justice.[111]

The upshot of this intricate opinion is that, while private persons are required to show actual malice in order to win a privacy case, in Pennsylvania they do not have to show subjective state of mind to demonstrate actual malice, and they

---

[111] *Uhl*, 476 F.Supp. at 1141.

do not have to use outtakes if the invasion of privacy takes place on television.

Five years before Prosser's definitive article on privacy was published an important early privacy case originated in Pittsburgh. Shortly after David Jenkins was kicked to death by a gang of youths, journalists from the Pittsburgh *Post-Gazette* and the Pittsburgh *Press* requested and received permission to take photographs from Agnes Jenkins, his widow. The photos were then sent by the *PostGazette* to the Association Press, which, through its World Wide Photos, Inc., affiliate, sold them to Dell. Dell then published them in its magazine entitled *Front Page Detective*, accompanied by a 150 word, accurate, factual account of the attack on David Jenkins. Agnes Jenkins sued Dell, saying the photographs in *Front* Page *Detective* caused her and her children "mental distress, embarrassment, and damage."[112]

The federal district court of the western district of Pennsylvania recognized two defenses for Dell. One is consent. The court observed, "They [Agnes Jenkins and her children] consented to be come actors in an occurrence of public interest; they voluntarily attached themselves pictorially to this news item."[113] The second defense recognized by this court was the newsworthiness privilege. The publication of the photographs, asserted the court, "did not unreasonably or seriously interfere with plaintiffs' [the Jenkins'] interest in not having the family picture exhibited to the public."[114] Although the court did not use the term false light, its reference to "fictionized" accounts is relevant to this form of privacy. The court said that "a false, fictionized, or dramatized account of the event or of the family" probably would have defeated the newsworthiness

---

[112] *Jenkins v. Dell Publishing Company,* 143 F.Supp 952, 954 (W.D.Pa. 1956).

[113] *Jenkins,* 143 F.Supp, 955.

[114] *Jenkins,* 143 F.Supp, 955.

justification.[115] It took care to distinguish the photographs and cutline from "cases where newsworthy events and accompanying pictures are distorted, fictionized, garnished, ridiculed, or falsified."[116]

These issues are refined importantly by a federal appeals court two years later.[117] First, the appeals court issued an important ruling related to the definition of news in a privacy case. The district court had accepted the Jenkins distinction between informational news and entertainment-oriented news. This distinction is rejected by the appeals court, "Once the character of an item as news is established, it is neither feasible nor desirable for a court to make a distinction between news for information and news for entertainment in determining" the newsworthiness privilege of privacy.[118] It continued, "For the purposes of the law of privacy we cannot see how the character of the item can be affected by the journal in which it appears. We conclude ... that the pictorially illustrated story ... is within the privilege which protects normal news items against claims of tortious invasion of privacy."[119]

Because it recognized a newsworthiness privilege, the appeals court avowedly avoided the consent defense, prompting a significant dissenting opinion. The dissent asserted that, because the consent given was only "a limited authorization" to publish the photographs in the local newspapers, publication in the magazine "grossly exceeded" the consent given by Agnes Jenkins and her children.[120] It also took care to note that the fact that the photograph was taken in the home and not in a public place makes consent an absolute necessity.

---

[115] *Jenkins,* 143 F.Supp, 955.
[116] *Jenkins,* 143 F.Supp, 955.
[117] *Jenkins v. Dell Publishing Company,* 251 F.2d 447 (3rd Cir. 1958).
[118] *Jenkins,* 251 F.2d, 451.
[119] *Jenkins,* 251 F.2d, 452.
[120] *Jenkins,* 251 F.2d, 454.

In short, the Pennsylvania courts seems to be saying that, once a private event becomes newsworthy, it tends to stay newsworthy and so the newsworthiness justification continues for a lengthy, if indefinite, period. If the re-circulation of a event is clearly not newsworthy, however, then even if consent was given for the original dissemination, this consent does not necessarily support unnewsworthy re-circulation.

Michael Santillo also included false light claim, but it too failed because he was unable to show the highly offensive statements about him were false and were publicized knowing they were not true or with reckless disregard of their falsity. He claimed that, although the published news story may have presented literally accurate discrete statements, the entire context of the story implied falsities. In order to prevail, though, the courts said he must show what it called discriminate publication of true statements. In other words, he must show that the publicity must have created a false impression by knowingly or recklessly publicizing selective pieces of true information. He attempted to do this by asserting that the department did not release information showing that he received commendations as a police officer. This assertion, the court said, misapprehends the meaning of discriminate publication.

Actual malice also tripped up another defendant in a false light case.[121] Bobby Seale sought damages from Gramercy Pictures, PolyGram Filmed Entertainment Distribution, Inc., Working Title Group, Inc., and Tribeca Productions, Inc. for the production, release, and distribution of the motion picture "Panther." He claimed the their portrayal of him in the film placed him in a false light.

Seale based his claim in part on a scene depicting a confrontation between him and Eldridge Cleaver. In this scene, the actors who play the roles of Seale and Cleaver engage in a

---

[121] *Seale v. Gramercy Pictures*, 964 F. Supp. 918 (E.D. Pa. 1997).

verbal confrontation, in the presence of other armed Black Panther party members and Little Bobby Hutton, over the role that violence should play in the party's activities following the assassination of Martin Luther King, Jr.. Seale contended the scene falsely depicts him as losing his control and leadership of the Black Panther party to Eldridge Cleaver and that it falsely depicts his relationship with Little Bobby Hutton because the scene shows Hutton rejecting Seale's guidance by leaving the confrontation. The court agreed. It found that the portrayal of Seale in the Confrontation scene, as well as their failure to include in the film a portrayal of Seale's leadership at the April 7, 1968, rally where he urged the Black Panther party members to return to their homes and to only use their guns in self-defense, does not depict him in the light he deserves.

As a public figure, however, Seale cannot prevail unless he can prove by clear and convincing evidence that the Gramercy Pictures portrayed him falsely with actual malice, i.e., the company knew it was portraying him in a false light or it portrayed him with false light out of a reckless disregard of whether it was false or not. Doing so out of mere negligence is not enough. Not only was Seale unable to show actual malice, he was unable to show negligence because the court said the evidence demonstrates that the defendants undertook substantial efforts to ensure the historical accuracy of the film's depiction of Seale when they retained the services of two consultants to work on the film's production--Tarika Lewis, who was the first woman to join the Black Panther party and Ula Taylor, Ph.D., an Assistant Professor of African-American Studies at the University of California at Berkeley.

The right of publicity is another aspect of privacy that was addressed by the court in this case. Seale said the use of his likeness in two photographs appearing on the brochure to the musical CD soundtrack was unauthorized   In response, the court boldly entered uncharted territory after pointing out that in 1997 there was no Pennsylvania case law clearly setting forth the elements for a right of publicity claim in Pennsylvania. Therefore, it predicted that the Pennsylvania Supreme Court will clarify the law concerning the right of publicity in Pennsylvania by adopting the *Restatement (Third) of Unfair Competition*, which was recently published by the American Law Institute in 1995. This revision requires Seale to present a preponderance of evidence that the defendants' use of the two photographs of the actor who played the role of Seale in the film was done solely to attract attention to a work that is not related to Seale. Since he did not do so, the court rejected his claim.

Intrusion

Intrusion upon the seclusion or solitude of a persons is the fourth form of privacy recognized by *Restatement of the Law: Torts*. The intrusion must be substantial, which means knocking on someone's door or calling them on the telephone does not qualify.

The intrusion type of privacy in recent years has focused increasingly on technological means of intruding into physical space and conversations. An important, relevant 2001 United States Supreme Court opinion has its roots in an event that took place in Pennsylvania.[122] During contentious collective-bargaining negotiations between a union representing teachers at the Wyoming Valley West High School and its school board, an unidentified person intercepted and recorded a cell phone conversation between the chief union negotiator and the teacher's union president. Frederick W. Vopper, a.k.a. Fred Williams, a radio commentator, played a tape of the intercepted conversation on his public affairs talk show as part of a series of news reports about the settlement. The union president filed suit under both federal and state wiretapping laws, alleging, among other things, that the conversation was illegally obtained and that Vopper repeatedly had published the conversation even

---

[122] Bartnicki v. Vopper, 532 U.S. 514 (2001).

though he knew or had reason to know that it had been intercepted illegally.

The Court said it accepted the claim that the interception was intentional and therefore unlawful, and that, at a minimum, Vopper "had reason to know" that it was unlawful, and it accepted the argument, that, therefore, disclosure of the contents of the intercepted conversation to representatives of the media, as well as the disclosures by the media to the public, violated both federal and state statutes. The only question left for the Court to answer, consequently, is whether the application of these statutes in such circumstances violates the First Amendment.[123]

The Court further said it accepted the following three allegations as facts. First, the media defendants played no part in the illegal interception. Rather, they found out about the interception only after it occurred, and in fact never learned the identity of the person or persons who made the interception. Second, their access to the information on the tapes was obtained lawfully, even though the information itself was intercepted unlawfully by someone else. Third, the subject matter of the conversation was a matter of public concern. If the statements about the labor negotiations had been made in a public arena--during a bargaining session, for example--they would have been newsworthy.[124] In spite of all these admissions, the Court ruled unconstitutional that part of both the federal and state laws that prohibited disclosures. It said that a prohibition against disclosure "is fairly characterized as a regulation of pure speech. Unlike the prohibition against the 'use' of the contents of an illegal interception."[125]

The Government identifies two interests, said the Court, served by the statute: first, the interest in removing an incentive

---

[123] Bartnicki, 532 U.S. at 525.
[124] Bartnicki, 532 U.S. at 525.
[125] Bartnicki, 532 U.S. at 526.

for parties to intercept private conversations, and, second, the interest in minimizing the harm to persons whose conversations have been illegally intercepted. Once again it accepted the argument that those interests adequately justify a prohibition against the interceptor's own use of information that he or she acquired by violating a statute, but it rejected the arguments that, therefore, punishing disclosures of lawfully obtained information of public interest by one not involved in the initial illegality is an acceptable means of serving those legitimate ends.[126] Writes the Court, "But it would be quite remarkable to hold that speech by a law-abiding possessor of information can be suppressed in order to deter conduct by a non-law-abiding third party."[127]

Additional attention from the Pennsylvania legislature and courts given to intrusion is discussed in the chapter on trespass.

---

[126] Bartnicki, 532 U.S. at 529.
[127] Bartnicki, 532 U.S. at 529.

Chapter 5

Obscenity Law

By Kathleen K. Olson

Introduction

Sex sells. Pornography, in the form of books, magazines, movies and Web sites, is big business, accounting for at least $2.6 billion annually in the United States.[1] At the same time, obscenity statutes restrict the content of sexually explicit materials, as they have since colonial times when harsh laws monitored public morality. While early Pennsylvania common law and statutes strictly prohibited "indecent, lewd and obscene" materials,[2] current law is guided by a number of United States Supreme Court decisions that established rules to ensure that obscenity laws do not run afoul of the First Amendment.

According to the U.S. Supreme Court, legally "obscene" materials do not enjoy First Amendment protection; they may be banned and their authors and distributors may be held criminally liable. An understanding of the legal test for obscenity is therefore essential to understanding state statutes regulating sexual materials.

Creating an exact definition of obscenity has been a difficult task for the courts; after all, "one man's vulgarity is

---

[1] Dan Ackman, *How Big is Porn?* Forbes.com (May 25, 2001), *available at* http://www.forbes.com/2001/05/25/0524porn.html
[2] 1860, March 31, P.L. 382, No. 374, sec. 40.

another man's lyric."[3] Obscene is not the same as "indecent," which is a legal standard used mainly in broadcasting and which may incorporate offensive but non-sexual material. Obscene is likewise not the same as "pornographic," a word that lacks legal meaning. In 1964, U.S. Supreme Court Justice Potter Stewart admitted that formulating a precise definition for obscenity was challenging but remarked, "I know it when I see it."[4]

Defining obscenity

The definition of obscenity has evolved over time as American courts have moved from using the broadly drawn *Hicklin* test of English common law to employing more specific definitions crafted to ban "hard core" pornography while protecting expression that is artistic or otherwise socially beneficial. The U.S. Supreme Court in the 1957 landmark case *Roth v. United States* ruled that obscene materials do not enjoy First Amendment protection but rejected the common law *Hicklin* test for determining whether a work is obscene. The *Hicklin* test defined obscenity based on the material's impact on children or other susceptible people and allowed an entire work to be declared obscene if a small portion of the work was obscene.[5] In *Roth*, the Court rejected this test and fashioned a new one. The proper test for obscenity, the Court said, was whether the work, taken as a whole and judged by the average person applying contemporary community standards, appealed to the "prurient" interest; that is, to a morbid, lascivious or unnatural interest in sex.[6]

The Court decided a number of obscenity cases after its *Roth* decision as it tried to clarify its new definition and answer some of the questions it had raised. By 1973, the political

---

[3] *Cohen v. California*, 403 U.S. 15, 25 (1971) (discussing four-letter expletive).
[4] *Jacobellis v. Ohio*, 378 U.S. 184 (1964) (Stewart, J., concurring).
[5] *Regina v. Hicklin*, L.R. 3 Q.B. 360 (1868).
[6] *Roth v. United States*, 354 U.S. 476 (1957).

makeup of the Court had changed significantly and, as a result, the Court in *Miller v. California* revisited its *Roth* standard and replaced it with a new obscenity test, which remains in effect today. As in the *Roth* test, obscenity depends on an analysis of the entire work by the "average person" applying contemporary community standards. The *Miller* test goes further, however. To be obscene, the following must be shown:

1. The average person, applying contemporary community standards, would find that the work, taken as a whole, appeals to the prurient interest; and
2. The work depicts or describes in a "patently offensive way," sexual conduct specifically defined by the applicable state law; and
3. The work, taken as a whole, lacks "serious literary, artistic, political, or scientific value."[7]

In *Miller*, therefore, the Court clarified the constitutional limits of governmental power to regulate obscene materials. The reformulated obscenity test was crafted to ensure that serious works would not be targeted by local prosecutors while at the same time allowing for the application of local standards of acceptable sexual expression.

Obscenity law in Pennsylvania

The *Miller* decision required states to reexamine their own obscenity laws, and Pennsylvania was no exception. Several Pennsylvania courts found that the Pennsylvania obscenity laws, as written, did not meet the three-part *Miller* test, primarily because of the second prong of the test, which requires that statutes clearly state what type of sexual expression is prohibited. This element is important since it provides notice to individuals as to what particular type of sexual depictions may result in criminal sanctions, thereby

---

[7] *Miller v. California*, 413 U.S. 15 (1973).

lessening the chance of a "chilling effect" on sexual expression in general.

In 1974, for example, the Pennsylvania Superior Court overturned the conviction of a Philadelphia go-go dancer for "obscene exhibition." The court found that because the Pennsylvania statute did not specifically describe what type of conduct was prohibited during a "public entertainment type exhibition," it failed the second part of the *Miller* test and was unconstitutional.[8] In another case decided shortly after *Miller* involving X-rated movies, the Court of Common Pleas threw out a criminal complaint filed against the films' exhibitors. The Pennsylvania Supreme Court affirmed, ruling that Pennsylvania's obscenity statute was unconstitutionally vague. The statute, the court said, "fails to satisfy the Miller standard and therefore may not constitutionally be applied unless and until it is amended to specifically define the sexual conduct whose depiction or description is to be regulated thereby."[9]

In several subsequent cases, Pennsylvania courts reiterated that the obscenity statute was unconstitutional as written,[10] and in 1977 the state legislature amended the obscenity statute to comply with *Miller*. The definition of "obscene" was changed to mirror the language of the *Miller* test and the revised statute withstood a series of constitutional challenges in the early 1980s.[11] The types of sexual conduct prohibited by the state are described, as required by the second *Miller* prong, as follows:

> Patently offensive representations or descriptions
> of ultimate sexual acts, normal or perverted,

---

[8] *Commonwealth v. Winkleman*, 326 A.2d 496 (Pa.Super. 1974).

[9] *Commonwealth v. MacDonald*, 347 A.2d 290 (Pa. 1975).

[10] See, for example, *Commonwealth v. Krasner*, 357 A.2d 558 (Pa.Super. 1976); *Commonwealth v. Van Emburg*, 359 A.2d 178 (Pa. 1976).

[11] *Commonwealth v. Bond*, 504 A.2d 869, 875 (Pa.Super. 1986) (listing cases).

actual or simulated, including sexual intercourse, anal or oral sodomy and sexual bestiality; and patently offensive representations or descriptions of masturbation, excretory functions, sadomasochistic abuse and lewd exhibition of the genitals.[12]

Pennsylvania law therefore makes it illegal for anyone, "knowing the obscene character of the materials or performances involved," to "sell, lend, distribute, exhibit, give away or show any obscene materials to any person 18 years of age or older."[13] A jury may infer the knowledge requirement by the circumstances, *e.g.*, that the materials were labeled "hard core" or were sold in an adult bookstore.[14] The law also makes it illegal to "design, copy, draw, photograph, print, utter, publish" or otherwise manufacture or prepare obscene materials or to "produce, present or direct any obscene performance."[15]

It is illegal to possess obscene materials with the intent to sell, lend, distribute, transmit, exhibit or give away or show them.[16] It is not illegal, however, to possess obscene materials in the privacy of one's own home without the intent to further distribute them. Following U.S. Supreme Court precedent, the Pennsylvania Superior Court ruled in *Commonwealth v. Stock* that, while the statute makes it illegal to "show" obscene materials, the law "should not be read so broadly as to take within its sweep mere private showings of obscene materials between consenting couples in their homes."[17] "The evil sought to be controlled by the statute," the court said, "is not the mere

---

[12] 18 *Pa.C.S.A.* 5903(b).
[13] 18 *Pa.C.S.A.* 5903(a). Separate provisions of the statute deal with minors. See, for example, 18 *Pa.C.S.A.* 5903(c).
[14] *Commonwealth v. Krasner*, 67 D.&C. 2d 171, 175-6 (1974).
[15] 18 *Pa.C.S.A.* 5903(a).
[16] 18 *Pa.C.S.A.* 5903(a).
[17] *Commonwealth v. Stock*, 499 A.2d 308, 312 (Pa.Super. 1985).

possession or even the showing of obscene materials in private, but the commercial exploitation of such materials, or at the very least their exhibition in a public setting where the individual's right to privacy is not a significant factor."[18]

Whether a given work is legally obscene is generally left to the jury to determine, and expert testimony is not required in order for the state to prove that the material appeals "to the prurient interest" or otherwise meets the definition of obscenity under the statute.[19] At the same time, however, courts have held, as a matter of law, that profane or vulgar expressions and language are not obscene,[20] nor is "mere nudity" without proof of additional sexual conduct.[21]

Nude dancing raises a separate legal issue than "mere" nudity because it contains an expressive element and may therefore implicate free speech interests. Nude dancing in Erie was the topic of litigation that reached the U.S. Supreme Court in 2000. The case, *City of Erie v. Pap's A.M.*, involved an ordinance passed by the city of Erie that made it a summary offense to appear in a public place in a "state of nudity."[22] The purpose of the ordinance was to restrict nude dancing clubs within the city, and the definition of "public place" included places of adult entertainment. The owner of the Kandyland strip club sued the city, arguing that the ordinance violated the First Amendment. The case reached the Pennsylvania Supreme Court, which struck down the ordinance as a violation of the First Amendment.[23] The case was appealed to the U.S.

---

[18] *Commonwealth v. Stock*, 313.

[19] *Commonwealth v. McCool*, 563 A.2d 901, 904-905 (Pa.Super. 1989).

[20] *Commonwealth v. Hock*, 728 A.2d 943 (Pa. 1999) (uttering profanities to police officer not "obscene"); *Brockway v. Shepherd*, 942 F. Supp. 1012 (M.D. Pa. 1996) (display of middle finger not "obscene").

[21] *Commonwealth v. Lebo*, 795 A.2d 987 (Pa.Super. 2002).

[22] *City of Erie v. Pap's A.M.*, 529 U.S. 277, 283 (2000).

[23] *Pap's A.M. v. City of Erie*, 719 A.2d 273 (Pa. 1998).

Supreme Court, which, in a plurality opinion, ruled that the ordinance did not violate the First Amendment.

According to the Court, nude dancing is considered "expressive conduct" and is generally entitled to First Amendment protection. However, because it is not "pure speech" (such as a book or a painting), the free-speech interests in nude dancing must be weighed against the government's interests in restricting such conduct. In this case, the Court said, the city's stated reason for the ban was to combat negative secondary effects of nude dancing clubs such as increased violence, sexual harassment, public intoxication and prostitution. The Court found that this was a legitimate interest that was unrelated to suppression of the expression itself. Because the ordinance was a "content-neutral" regulation that furthered an important governmental interest unrelated to the expression, and because the restriction did not restrict speech any more than was necessary, it did not violate the First Amendment.[24]

The U.S. Supreme Court's decision was not the end of the Kandyland case, however, because the case was remanded to the Pennsylvania Supreme Court for further proceedings. The Pennsylvania court took the opportunity to abandon First Amendment-based analysis and turn instead to the Pennsylvania Constitution as support for its renewed decision to strike down the ordinance. The state constitution, the court said, provides even greater protection for freedom of expression than the U.S. Constitution. The court relied on the text and history of Article I, Section 7 of the state constitution, saying, "The provision is

---

[24] *City of Erie v. Pap's A.M.,* 529 U.S. 277, 296-302 (2000). The Court subjected the ordinance to intermediate scrutiny using the *O'Brien* test for determining whether government regulation of expressive conduct is unconstitutional. See *United States v. O'Brien,* 391 U.S. 367 (1968) (burning a draft card not protected speech).

an ancestor, not a stepchild, of the First Amendment."[25] The court also stated its belief that it should "tread carefully" where restraints are imposed on commercial speech if less intrusive methods are available to further governmental interests. Because the court believed that was the case in Erie, it struck down the ordinance as a violation of the Pennsylvania Constitution.

In this case, therefore, the Pennsylvania Supreme Court's interpretation of state law proved more protective of free expression than the U.S. Supreme Court's First Amendment analysis. The state court's ruling did not cause another look at the obscenity statutes on the books, however. Indeed, Pennsylvania courts had previously rejected the argument that the Pennsylvania Constitution afforded greater protection to obscene materials than the First Amendment and the Kandyland decision did nothing to change that view.[26]

Minors and obscenity

Courts have traditionally been much more protective of children than adults when it comes to regulating obscenity, both with regard to what children can read or view and their participation in the creation of pornography. The U.S. Supreme Court has acknowledged that states have a compelling interest in protecting the welfare of children so that a different standard of obscenity is permitted when creating rules for minors.

Thus the Pennsylvania obscenity law prohibits the dissemination of "explicit sexual materials" to minors (those under the age of 18). It makes it illegal to knowingly display such materials in any commercial establishment or in such a

---

[25] *Pap's A.M. v. City of Erie*, 812 A.2d 591, 606 (Pa. 2002) (ruling that Article I, Section 7 is broader than the First Amendment because it "specifically affirms the 'invaluable right' to the 'free communication of thoughts and opinions.'").

[26] See, for example, *Commonwealth v. Croll*, 480 A.2d 266, 269 (Pa.Super. 1984); *In re Condemnation (Appeal of New Garden Theatre)*, No. 65 C.D. 1999, No. 1063 C.D. 2002 (Pa.Commw. 2003).

manner that the display is visible from a public place where minors may be exposed to them.[27] "Explicit sexual materials" are materials that are obscene or are visual representations of the human body that depict "nudity, sexual conduct, or sadomasochistic abuse" and are "harmful to minors." Explicit sexual materials may also consist of written material containing similar depictions or explicit descriptions of "sexual excitement, sexual conduct, or sadomasochistic abuse" which, taken as a whole, are "harmful to minors."[28] The law makes it illegal to knowingly admit a minor to a film or show that depicts nudity, sexual conduct or sadomasochistic abuse and which is "harmful to minors," unless the minor is accompanied by a parent.[29]

What is considered "harmful to minors"? The Pennsylvania statute's definition is nearly identical to the obscenity standard, except that it takes into consideration the vulnerability of minors. Something is "harmful to minors" if it predominantly appeals to the prurient interest of minors, is patently offensive to prevailing standards in the adult community with respect to what is suitable for minors, and, if taken as a whole, lacks serious literary, artistic, political, education or scientific value for minors.[30] Thus something that would not be considered obscene for adults may be considered harmful to minors and restricted to adults only. These special considerations in the law for minors found support from the U.S. Supreme Court in 1968, when the Court ruled that states may adopt more restrictive obscenity rules for minors than for adults and upheld a New York law that was nearly identical to the Pennsylvania statute regarding materials "harmful to minors."[31]

---

[27] 18 *Pa.C.S.A.* 5903(a)(1).
[28] 18 *Pa.C.S.A.* 5903(c).
[29] 18 *Pa.C.S.A.* 5903(d).
[30] 18 *Pa.C.S.A.* 5903(e)(6).
[31] See *Ginsberg v. New York*, 390 U.S. 629 (1968).

Both federal and state laws exist that seek to protect children from exploitation in the creation of pornography. While the First Amendment protects an adult's right to possess obscene materials in the privacy of one's own home, the same is not true with regard to materials depicting minors performing sexual acts.[32] The U.S. Supreme Court has ruled that child pornography may be banned by states even if the material does not meet the legal test for obscenity in order to protect minors from exploitation.[33]

The Pennsylvania obscenity law makes it illegal to "hire, employ, use or permit" any minor child (under the age of 18) to participate in any act prohibited by the statute.[34] In 2002, however, the Pennsylvania Superior Court made clear that the safeguards built into the obscenity test apply to cases involving the exploitation of minors as well. The court threw out obscenity charges against a photographer who had taken photos of nude and partially clothed 16- and 17-year-old girls. Because "mere nudity is not obscenity," and because the photographs did not depict sexual acts, "overtly sexual or lewd poses" or the girls' genitals, the court found that the statute's definition of obscenity had not been met and the defendant's obscenity convictions were overturned.[35]

Obscenity and the Internet

Numerous legislative attempts have been made to protect minors from the proliferation of pornography on the Internet, although most have been criticized as overreaching violations of adults' First Amendment rights. The federal laws regulating Internet content are of interest not only because they are enforceable in Pennsylvania but because constitutional

---

[32] *Osborne v. Ohio*, 495 U.S. 103 (1990) (upholding Ohio statute making it illegal to possess child pornography).

[33] *New York v. Ferber*, 458 U.S. 747 (1982) (involving materials in which children under the age of 16 performed sexual acts).

[34] 18 *Pa.C.S.A.* 5903(a)(6).

[35] *Commonwealth v. Lebo*, 795 A.2d 987, 991-992 (Pa.Super. 2002).

challenges have been brought in federal court in Philadelphia against each one:

- **The Communications Decency Act (CDA):** Part of the Telecommunications Act of 1996, this statute attempted to ban "indecent" material from Internet sites accessible by minors. In 1997, the U.S. Supreme Court affirmed the decision of the U.S. District Court for the Eastern District of Pennsylvania that overturned parts of the law, including the prohibition on public displays of pornography and other material considered "indecent." The Court ruled that the Internet must be afforded the broad First Amendment protections given to print materials rather than the stricter regulatory control permissible for broadcasting.[36]

- **The Child Online Protection Act:** Signed into law in 1998, this statute was an attempt to craft a narrower law after the CDA was struck down by the U.S. Supreme Court. The statute banned material "harmful to minors" from commercial Web sites accessible to minors. The Third Circuit struck down the law in 2000, stating that the law and current technology could not constitutionally prevent access by minors to Web sites without also infringing on adults' rights to access those sites.[37] The U.S. Supreme Court upheld some portions of the law but sent the case back to the Third Circuit in 2002 for further consideration of the First Amendment issues involved.[38]

---

[36] *American Civil Liberties Union v. Reno*, 521 U.S. 844 (1997).

[37] *American Civil Liberties Union v. Reno*, 217 F.3d 162 (3d Cir. 2000).

[38] *Ashcroft v. American Civil Liberties Union*, 535 U.S. 564 (2002).

- **The Children's Internet Protection Act:** This act required public libraries receiving federal funds to install and use Internet filtering software to block Web sites deemed "harmful to minors." In *America Library Association v. United States*, the federal district court in Philadelphia ruled the statute unconstitutional because filters block constitutionally protected speech, including information on political and health issues, as well as the targeted material.[39] In June 2003, the U.S. Supreme Court upheld the law, ruling in a plurality opinion that the statute was not an abuse of Congress' powers to control how federal funds are used and did not violate adult library patrons' First Amendment rights.[40]

Federal laws have also targeted the exploitation of minors in the creation of pornography, most recently by prohibiting digitally "morphed" images that are made to appear as if children are engaging in sexual activities. Congress passed amended legislation to target these materials in 2003 after the Supreme Court struck down an earlier attempt, the Child Pornography Prevention Act, as being unconstitutionally overbroad.[41]

Pennsylvania law and the Internet

Regulation of the Internet has been left primarily to the federal government, although Pennsylvania has recently taken steps toward regulation that have dismayed businesses and civil libertarians alike. In 2002, the Pennsylvania legislature passed a statute that requires Internet service providers (ISPs) to remove or disable access to child pornography materials

---

[39] *American Library Association, Inc. v. United States*, 201 F.Supp. 2d 401 (E.D. Pa. 2002).

[40] *United States v. American Library Association, Inc.*, No. 02-361 (June 23, 2003).

[41] *Ashcroft v. Free Speech Coalition*, 535 U.S. 234 (2002).

residing on their servers or accessible through their services.[42] The law requires ISPs doing business in Pennsylvania to block child pornography sites wherever they may be located and without regard to whether there is any business relationship or other connection between the site and the ISP. ISPs are not required to search for or monitor child pornography sites, but they must remove or block sites that are referred to them by the state Attorney General or a district attorney within five days. Penalties for non-compliance with orders to remove a site can run from $5,000 to $30,000 plus up to seven years in jail.[43]

The law is the only one of its kind in the nation. ISPs and civil liberties groups have objected to the statute because it sets up a process of judicial review that allows the Attorney General to get court approval to ban a Web site without notice or an opportunity for a hearing as to whether the site actually contains child pornography. In addition, according to the statute, an "Internet Service Provider" is "a person who provides a service that enables users to access content, information, electronic mail or other services offered over the Internet."[44] Under this definition, libraries, schools or other establishments offering Internet access may be targeted under the statute.

In the year following the effective date of the statute, Attorney General Mike Fisher bypassed the mandated judicial process altogether and forced the blocking of more than 400 Internet sites by informal order. Internet service provider WorldCom Inc. objected to the statute's reach in September 2002, arguing that technological limitations had forced the company to block the sites from all of its North American subscribers in order to comply with the Pennsylvania statute.[45]

---

[42] 18 *Pa.C.S.A.* 7621-7629.

[43] 18 *Pa.C.S.A.* 7623-7624.

[44] 18 *Pa.C.S.A.*7621.

[45] Charles Thompson, *Montgomery County, Pa., Judge Orders WorldCom to Block Porn Sites*, The [Harrisburg] Patriot-News (September 19, 2002).

A Montgomery County judge rejected the ISP's argument and ordered the company to obey an order to deny access to five sites. The Center for Technology and Democracy explored the possibility of filing a legal challenge to the statute in the spring of 2003 and requested a list of the sites that had been ordered blocked, but the Attorney General's office refused to disclose that information.[46]

---

[46] Associated Press, *Pa. refuses to identify Web sites blocked in child-porn sweep* (April 24, 2003).

Chapter 6

Trespass

By Douglas S. Campbell

Under British common law, trespass was a very broad concept. It represented all actions taken to recover damages for injuries to a person's body, a person's land, or a person's relationships with another human being.[1] The most common notion of trespass in the late twentieth century, however, is what was known under common law as trespass quare clausum fregit (because he [or she] broke the close). It is sometimes called trespass upon land.

Put simply, trespass is an unauthorized entry upon another person's land. This form of trespass should be treated with great delicacy by journalists because no actual injury or damage must occur in order for trespass legally to have taken place. Nor it is necessary that a person actually step onto the land. Throwing a baseball over a neighbor's property or even flying an airplane over the property of another can, in certain circumstances, constitute trespass.

Today, trespass falls under both criminal and civil law. The primary purpose of criminal trespass, the courts have ruled, is to prevent breaches of the peace.[2] One judge described the difference this way: "The primary objective is to exclude

---

[1] Black's Law Dictionary, 1502 (7th ed. 1996). For a cursory historical survey of the origins of trespass law see *Commonwealth v. Everhart*, 57 Pa. Super 192 (1914).

[2] *Commonwealth v. White*, 492 A.2d 32, 36 (Pa.Super. 1985).

criminal prosecution for mere presence of a person in a place where the public generally is invited."[3]

Persons are criminal trespassers if they secretly or deceptively enter an "occupied structure" without a license or privileged to do so. According to the definition found in the Pennsylvania Crimes Code of an "occupied structure," another person does not have to be present in a structure for a building to be considered occupied. The building is considered occupied if a "structure" (including a motor vehicle) is "adapted for overnight accommodation or for carrying on business."[4]

If, in addition to entering, persons were to break into a structure, then the penalty is more severe. The Crimes Code defines "breaking into" as gaining "entry by force ... intimidation, unauthorized opening of locks, or through an opening not designed for human access."[5]

Finally, when persons trespass in spite of obvious warnings not to--such as no trespass signs, a fence, or a verbal objection--then these persons become defiant trespassers. Defiant trespass is a misdemeanor of the third degree when persons defy "an order to leave personally communicated" to them "by the owner of the premises or another authorized person."[6] Otherwise it is a summary offense.[7]

The law provides some rather commonsense defenses for criminal trespass. A defense does not necessarily mean persons can trespass lawfully. It means only that trespassers can use the defense to assert their right to be present. The first

---

[3] *White*, 492 A.2d 32 at 35. The Pennsylvania Supreme Court asserted in *Commonwealth v. Thomas*, 561 A.2d 699 (Pa. 1989) that the "basic element of crime of criminal trespass is an unprivileged entry, the same element as in crime of burglary. "

[4] 18 Pa. Conn. Stat. Ann. § 3501 (2002).

[5] 18 Pa. Conn. Stat. Ann. § 3503.a.3. (2002)

[6] 18 Pa. Conn. Stat. Ann. § 3503.b.2. (2002)

[7] In Pennsylvania the maximum fine for a summary offense is $300 and the maximum prison term is 90 days. A third degree misdemeanor conviction carries a maximum fine of $2,500 and a maximum prison term of one year.

defense is that the building or premises were open to the public and the trespasser complied with all the lawful restrictions imposed on entering or remaining there.[8] A second is that the building was abandoned.[9] The third is that the trespasser reasonably believed (ultimately a judge or jury would decide if the belief is reasonable) that either the owner or someone with legal authority gave permission to enter or to remain.[10]

The primary defense for civil trespass is consent or authorization. Consent is not a simple concept, because the person who can give the consent in not easily identified. The law recognizes four forms of ownership of real property (land): ownership itself, possession, use, and control. Ownership is the core and often, but not necessarily, encompasses the other three. This aspect is ordinarily used when describing the rights of the person who holds title to a piece of real estate.

Possession refers to the general right to use the property during limited periods of possession; tenants or renters most frequently assert this aspect of ownership. Use usually takes the form of an easement, which can be described as a right of way; easements are given, for example, to utility companies to put and maintain a telephone or electrical pole on your property. Control can be granted to another person by the holder of title or by statutory law. The title holder of property upon which a restaurant in built, for example, could grant control to someone who manages the restaurant on a daily basis.

Seeking consent from an owner, therefore, may result in some frustration since the owner who has the legal right to grant authorization may not be determined easily. One of the most common errors related to consent arises when members of the general public enter a place of business.

---

[8] 18 Pa. Conn. Stat. Ann. § 3503.C.2 (2002).

[9] 18 Pa. Conn. Stat. Ann. § 3503.C. (2002).

[10] 18 Pa. Conn. Stat. Ann. § 3503.C.3 (2002).

Consent may appear to be implied when a journalist walks into a business establishment, such as a hardware store. Yet implied consent is limited, and the public has no legal right to exceed these limits. The case of *Sloan v. Schomaker* can be very sobering to journalists.[11] The Pennsylvania Supreme Court ruled that, when persons enter a store by implied permission, they have a duty when asked to leave to do so with reasonable speed. Moreover, if they do not leave, then the owner does not have to call the police, but can use reasonable force to eject them. Finally, the court asserted that, if the trespasser remains, then the owner is not responsible for the consequences (although the owner may not breach the peace to enforce an ejection).

More recently, this court ruled, "Even though a person has entered the business premises of another, at the invitation of the owner, his subsequent conduct may be such as to justify the revocation of the invitation to remain as a guest. The invitee, if he remains, then becomes a trespasser."[12] The court asserted that the owner of the business has the right to order such a trespasser from the premises, and, in case of refusal, has the additional right to remove that person by force if necessary.[13]

While it is true that the owner cannot always be certain at what point a guest becomes a trespasser, these fine points of law usually are not obviously apparent when journalists enter a business with notebook or television camera in hand. For example, a trial court ruled that a person was not a trespasser when the owner pointed a loaded gun before ordering a guest to leave the property.[14] This fine distinction revolves around

---

[11] *Sloan v. Schomaker*, 20 A. 525 (Pa. 1890); followed in *Horney v. Nixon*, 61 A. 1088 (Pa. 1905) and again in *Yoder v. Yoder*, 86A. 523 (Pa. 1913).
[12] *Commonwealth v. Johnston*, 263 A.2d 376, 379 (Pa.1970).
[13] *Johnston*, 263 A.2d at 379.
[14] *Brotzman v. Moser*, 56 Pa. D. & C.2d 286 (1971), aff'd, 294 A.2d 703 (Pa. Super 1972).

whether the gun is pointed before or after a person is ordered off a piece of property.

In addition, the court extended some of the rights previously associated only with the home to rights associated with businesses. An exception to the duty to retreat when faced with a physical threat was extended from the home to the business place.[15] It is possible, therefore, that the courts may also be willing to extend to the business place some of the other traditional notions of privacy associated with the home, thus strengthening the privacy rights of the business place.

The British common law rights of business owners to eject patrons--forcibly if necessary--from their place of business was given additional force in the United States by Judge Cooley in his highly influential late nineteenth-century book on *Torts*.[16] He writes, "A theatre ticket is a mere license to the purchaser which may be revoked at the pleasure of the theatrical manager, upon such revocation, if the person attempts to enter, or if, having previously entered, he refuses to leave upon request, he becomes a trespasser, and may be prevented from entering or may be removed by force, and can maintain no action of tort therefore"[17]

The Pennsylvania Supreme Court subsequently adopted the concept in 1905 when it ruled, "The proprietor of a theater is a private individual, engaged in a strictly private business, which, though for the entertainment of the public, is always limited to those whom he may agree to admit to it. There is no duty . . . to admit every one who may apply and be willing to pay for a ticket, for the theater proprietor . . . is . . . under no implied obligation to serve the public."[18] The court added

---

[15] *Johnston*, 263 A.2d at 380, see *Commonwealth v. Wilkes*, 199 A. 2d 411 (Pa. 1964), *cert. denied*, 379 U.S. 939 (1964).

[16] Second Edition, 306, quoted in *Horney v Nixon*, 61A. 1088, 1089 (Pa. 1905).

[17] *Horney*, 61 A. at 1089.

[18] *Horney*, 61 A. at 1089.

emphatically, "If the person attempts to enter, or if, having previously entered, he refuses to leave upon request, he becomes a trespasser, and may be prevented from entering or may be removed by force [emphasis added], and can maintain no action or tort, therefore."[19]

The right to remove a trespasser by force appears also in the Pennsylvania Crimes Code.[20] The statute reads in part as follows:

> The use of force upon or toward the person of another i8 justifiable [emphasis added] when the actor believes that such force is immediately necessary: (1) to prevent or terminate [emphasis added] an unlawful entry or other trespass upon land or tangible movable property, if such land or movable property is, or is believed by the actor to be, in his possession or in the possession of another person for whose protection he acts
> . . ..
> The use of force is justifiable under this section only if the actor first requests the person against whom such force is used to desist from his interference with the property, unless the actor believes that: (i) such request would be useless; (ii) it would be dangerous to himself or another person to make the request; or(iii) substantial harm will be done to the physical condition of the property which is sought to be protected before the request can effectively be made.[21]

---

[19] *Horney*, 61 A. at 1089.
[20] 18 Pa. Conn .Stat. Ann. § 507.
[21] 18 Pa. Conn .Stat. Ann. § 507.

A prudent journalist, therefore, would be well advised to leave, when order to so by someone who appears to be an owner or to have possession, any property that is not clearly open to the general public.

Parking lots may be more friendly grounds to journalists than buildings. At least parking lots appear to support the defense of consent when they are open to the public. A court ruled that persons can remain in parking lots as long as the lots are open to the general public and all lawful conditions to remain on the lot are obeyed, adding, somewhat paradoxically, that the public nature of a parking lot would make it "unlikely that any conditions" for remaining would be "lawful."[22] Abortion protesters discovered, though, that not all parking lots are equally open. A trial judge asserted, for example, "A single tenant of a multi-business establishment has the right to exclude those whom it chooses from the parking lot. The parking lot is not "open to the public" but is open merely for the use of business invitees.[23]

Journalists who may be tempted to discover some creative First Amendment defense, should be warned that, when abortion protesters attempted to use the defense of criminal justification, they failed.[24] The Pennsylvania Crimes code's section on justification as an affirmative defense reads in part, "Conduct which the actor believes to be necessary to avoid a harm or evil to himself or to another is justifiable if: (1) the harm or evil sought to be avoided by such conduct is greater than that sought to be prevented by the law defining the offense charged.[25] The protesters claimed that trespassing on the property of an abortion clinic is necessary and so justified in

---

[22] *Commonwealth v. Herlihy*, 42 Pa. D. & C.3d 545 (1987), *see Commonwealth v. White*. 492 A.2d 32 (Pa. Super. 1985).

[23] *Commonwealth v. Dow*, 3 Pa. D. & C.4th 283 (1989).

[24] *Northeast Women's Center, Inc. v. McMonagle*, 868 F.2d 1342 (3rd Cir. 1989).

[25] 18 Pa. Conn .Stat .Ann. § 503.

order to avoid the greater harm of abortion. The court ruled, however, that this defense was not available to them. It would appear, therefore, that journalists would have a difficult time justifying trespassing as the only alternative to avoiding a the greater threat of damage to the First Amendment or even to the public at large.

Journalists who might be tempted to trespass because they feel their unauthorized presence is justified by this same statute, would be well advised to review first the state's supreme court's interpretation it. Four tests must be passed, the court asserted, before the trespass satisfies statutory justification. It ruled that trespasses must be able to offer evidence that will demonstrate the following:

> (1) that the actor was faced with a clear and imminent harm, not one which is debatable or speculative;
>
> (2) that the actor could reasonably expect that the actor's actions would be effective in avoiding this greater harm;
>
> (3) that there is no legal alternative which will be effective in abating the harm; and
>
> (4) that the Legislature has not acted to preclude the defense by a clear and deliberate choice regarding the values at issue.[26]

Common sense may be a sufficient guide for journalists who face the possibility trespass. While private property is more clearly restricted than is public, the distinctions between the two are not always clear and the penalties for various forms and degrees of trespass can be substantial.

Distribution

One area of trespass directly germane to the media is the presence of newsstands and news boxes or news racks on public

---

[26] *Commonwealth v. Capitolo*, 498 A.2d 806, 809 (Pa. 1985), these four tests are also set forth in *Commonwealth v. Berrigan*, 501 A.2d 226, 229 (Pa. 1985).

sidewalks.[27] The distribution of newspapers has received substantial attention from the federal courts and some from Pennsylvania Courts. Whether regulations of newsstands and news boxes are constitutional depends upon a number of factors, but in Pennsylvania the Supreme Court issued its first important ruling on this topic in 1960 after the 46 South 52nd Street Corporation in Philadelphia attempted to have the newsstand operated by Oscar Manlin removed from its location because it stood directly in front of a newly remodeled show window.[28] The corporation based its case on ownership, saying the purpose of the easement taken by the city of Philadelphia is solely to facilitate passage of the public. Manlin based his case on custom, he had sold newspapers on that site since 1932, and an exception in a city ordinance.

The Court quickly dismissed the custom argument, saying simply, "Although the custom of having newsstands in Philadelphia has existed for approximately 100 years, this custom is not enough to warrant such continuance."[29] The exception to an ordinance required more attention. First, the court noted, "The commonwealth from an early date delegated to the City of Philadelphia broad power to permit and control reasonable encroachments upon the public sidewalks."[30] It also said Philadelphia could regulate newsstands under this authority even though the United States Supreme Court ruled more than twenty years earlier that "the sale and distribution of newspapers ... must be permitted on the sidewalks and

---

[27] Although court decisions sometimes combine the terms news box and news rack into one word, most dictionaries at present do not sanction this usage. Newsstand, in contrast, is an accepted word.

[28] *46 South 52nd Street Corporation v. Manlin*, 157 A.2d 381 (Pa. 1960).

[29] *46 South 52nd Street*, 157 A.2d at 387.

[30] *46 South 52nd Street*, 157 A.2d at 387. The court cited an nineteenth-century statute: 53 Pa. .Stat. Ann. § 16436 (1838).

highways of our nation.[31] Justice Cohen, writing for the court, stated, "And while it is true that a free press is essential to the maintenance of liberty, . . . it does not necessarily follow that a governmental body may not regulate for even prevent the use of stationary newsstands for that purpose. Newsstands are neither essential nor even necessary for the distribution of newspapers."[32]

Manlin claimed the ordinances protected the presence of his newsstands because the series of Philadelphia ordinances dating from 1931 and restricting sidewalk sales all contained an exemption for the sale of newspapers, books, and magazines. To the court the issue was not so obvious. Cohen wrote, "The question we now face directly is whether the exemption contained in these ordinances constitutes the requisite municipal sanction and a sufficient surrender of the public easement for a public use."[33] Answering its own question, the court said the exemption does not grant "express" permission to set newsstands on the sidewalks of Philadelphia. Instead, the exemption merely allows Manlin to apply for permission from the City of Philadelphia. Since Manlin had never expressly sought permission, he was ruled a trespasser.

In essence, the court said newsstands are a convenience, but not a necessity, because "the newspaper public can be adequately served by buying at nearby stores, hotels, stations, etc."[34] An important United States Supreme Court precedent cited, but not developed by the court, however, is a ruling that freedom of the press "must not in the guise of regulations, be abridged or denied."[35] This precedent becomes central more

---

[31] *46 South 52nd Street*, 157 A.2d at 386; *See Hague v. C.I.O.*, 307 U.S. 496 (1939).
[32] *46 South 52nd Street*, 157 A.2d at 387.
[33] *46 South 52nd Street*, 157 A.2d at 388.
[34] *46 South 52nd Street*, 157 A.2d at 387, 395.
[35] *46 South 52nd Street*, 157 A.2d at 386. *See Hague v. C.I.O.*, 307 U.S. 496 (1939).

than a decade later in a case that came before a federal district court hearing a case originating in Pennsylvania.[36]

Fearing "pervasive commercialism in our cities that is rapidly encroaching upon pleasant and well-ordered suburban communities," the borough of Swarthmore, on the avowed authority of its own resolution modifying a borough ordinance, removed two Philadelphia *Inquirer* news boxes from sidewalks within the borough limits. The borough presented to the Eastern Pennsylvania Federal District Court two primary arguments supporting its actions. First, it said the ordinances were not directed toward newspapers *per se*, but towards prohibiting commercial usage and preventing obstruction of public streets. Secondly, the *Inquirer* loses its First Amendment rights in this situation because it is a commercial enterprise as evidence by the facts that it is sold and not given away and that the content consists of approximately 45 per cent advertising.

Citing numerous persuasive precedents from other districts, the court responded by asserting that a newspaper does not lose its First Amendment protections simply "because it is operated for profit, or forms part of a profit-making enterprise."[37] After all, the court took notice, Thomas Paine did not distribute his pamphlets free of charge.[38]

Next, the court said, "Further, we are satisfied that the constitutional protection extends to *means* [emphasis in original] of distribution of the newspaper, as well as to its content and the ideas expressed therein."[39] It continued, "The right of access to the streets includes not only the right to speak freely, but the related right to distribute printed material."[40]

---

[36] *Philadelphia News, Inc., v. Borough C., etc., Swarthmore*, 381 F. Supp. 228 (E.D. Pa. 1974).
[37] *Philadelphia News, Inc.*, 381 F. Supp. at 239.
[38] *Philadelphia News, Inc.*, 381 F. Supp. at 240.
[39] *Philadelphia News, Inc.*, 381 F. Supp. at 240.
[40] *Philadelphia News, Inc.*, 381 F. Supp. at 242.

The problem, as the court saw it, was how to balance "the proper interest of the municipality in promoting the welfare of its citizens" against the benefits of freedom of expression; the answer was a "more narrowly drawn provision" that would eliminate the "feared evil" without threatening a free press."[41] Properly drawn regulations of time, place, and manner could be upheld the court noted.

It cited two examples: first, "If the feared evil is obstruction of the sidewalks that will interfere with the public's right to unhampered passage thereon, narrow regulations as to the size and location of the newspaper boxes could be formulated which would certainly survive constitutional scrutiny."[42] Secondly, "If the feared evil is traffic congestion or illegal parking or stopping by motorists in order to purchase newspapers, narrow regulations with respect to the location of newspapers boxes in relation to the character of the roadway could also be formulated" as long as "the existence of parking facilities, an adequate shoulder, etc.," also are taken into consideration.[43] Moreover, the court said that "aesthetic considerations could justify the promulgation of reasonable regulations as to the size and appearance of the boxes, and the type and format of permissible identification or advertising."[44] Referring to the United State Supreme Court precedent that was ignored by the Pennsylvania Supreme Court in 1960, the federal court asserted that "the fatal flaw in the ordinance and resolution" was that it was so broad it used "impermissible means to achieve permissible ends."[45]

It is interesting to note that the federal court, without citing the Pennsylvania Supreme Court decision, declared "irrelevant" the Pennsylvania court's observation that the

---

[41] *Philadelphia News, Inc.,* 381 F. Supp. at 242.
[42] *Philadelphia News, Inc.,* 381 F. Supp. at 244.
[43] *Philadelphia News, Inc.,* 381 F. Supp. at 244.
[44] *Philadelphia News, Inc.,* 381 F. Supp. at 244.
[45] *Philadelphia News, Inc.,* 381 F. Supp. at 244.

newspaper could be purchased at locations other than newsstands. Indeed, one very important aspect of this decision is an extension to newsstands of the United States Supreme Court's recognition of the existence of a right of access to public streets. The district court asserted forthrightly that newsstands are a of expression protected by the First Amendment. The other important aspect is the court's ruling that city ordinances designed to regulate newsstands must be so narrowly drawn that they do not threatened freedom of the press. While such regulations can be drawn said the court, for example, to ensure unobstructed passage on public sidewalks, or to eliminate traffic hazards, or even to enhance the aesthetic aura of the community, the regulations must not go beyond their intended purpose and, by being unconstitutionally broad, also threaten a free press in their zeal to combat a "feared evil."

The first important federal case[46] to address newsracks in public places arose from a neighboring state (New York) in 1984. Since Pennsylvania lies in the same circuit as New York, many of the issues in this case became central to six important future cases that either control or strongly influence Pennsylvania law.

The origin of this early case can be traced to April 4, 1983, when Gannett Satellite Information Network, Inc. sought permission from the Metropolitan Transportation Authority's (MTA) to place approximately 100 newsracks for *USA Today* in public areas of MTA stations. After the MTA sent to Gannett it's policy containing fees and conditions placed on newsracks , the publisher sued claiming that its right to distribute newspapers through newsracks was protected by the First and Fourteenth Amendments and that MTA's licensing scheme and fees violated these rights because (1) MTA had failed to establish standards to govern the issuance of licenses and so had

---

[46] *Gannett Satellite Information Network, Inc. v. Metropolitan Transportation Authority*, 745 F.2d 767 (2d Cir. 1984).

given its employees unlimited discretion in prohibiting or conditioning the placement of newsracks; (2) MTA's licensing fees were a tax singling out the press; and (3) MTA's licensing requirement and fees operated as a prior restraint.

The first issue addressed, but only briefly, was the notion of a forum, an idea that was vetted at length by the United States Supreme Court when ruling on a First Amendment issue arising from a high school.[47] The Court said there are two kinds of fora: public and private. Public fora can be either traditional or designated. The district court in the newsrack case said the public areas of MTA stations, although not traditional or designated public fora, are appropriate fora for newsrack distributions, and the Court of appeals, with little analysis, simply agreed. It wrote, "[w]e hold that the MTA stations are appropriate forums for the exercise of Gannett's First Amendment right to distribute its newspapers through newsracks."[48]

The second circuit said that, although neither a traditional nor a designated public forum, the MTA public areas still can serve as a forum for expression if the expression is appropriate for the property, and is not "incompatible with the normal activity of a particular place at a particular time."[49] These areas in fact are compatible, said the court, because thousands of commuters who pass through the stations each day provide a ready market for morning newspapers and because since at least 1965 several publishers have maintained newsracks in the stations.

Reaching back to the high school case again, the court said that even though the public areas of the MTA are appropriate fora, the MTA may impose reasonable time, place and manner restrictions on newsrack placement as long as the

---

[47] *Perry Education Ass'n v. Perry Local Educators' Ass'n*, 460 U.S. 37 (1983).
[48] *Gannett*, 745 F.2d 771.
[49] *Gannett*, 745 F.2d 773.

restrictions are justified without reference to the content of the regulated speech, they are narrowly tailored to serve a significant governmental interest, and they leave open ample alternative channels for communication of the information.[50]

Addressing the first condition, the court said the fees are content-neutral because they are imposed upon any newspaper desiring to install newsracks.[51] To the third condition, the court noted that, even if the licensing fees were so high that they rendered newsrack newspaper sales economically infeasible, Gannett would still have ample alternative means to distribute its newspapers to MTA commuters.[52] It could place newsracks on streets or sidewalks near the stations and it could use news pedestrian vendors or existing newsstands to sell its newspapers. Writes the court, "Although the alternative distribution method may be more costly, the First Amendment does not guarantee a right to the least expensive means of expression."[53]

The second condition, though, was a bit more complex. The court admitted, "Ordinarily, a government cannot profit by imposing licensing or permit fees on the exercise of a First Amendment right."[54] Allowable fees may cover only the administrative costs of the permit or license are permissible. This notion applies only when the government was acts in a governmental capacity and attempts to raising general revenue under the guise of defraying its administrative costs. When the government is engaged in commercial enterprise, such as managing a railroad station, the raising of revenue is a significant interest. Consequently, the licensing fees are permissible manner restrictions because they serve the

---

[50] *Gannett*, 745 F.2d 773. See also *Clark v. Community for Creative Non-Violence*, 468 U.S. 288 (1984).
[51] *Gannett*, 745 F.2d 773.
[52] *Gannett*, 745 F.2d 774.
[53] *Gannett*, 745 F.2d 774.
[54] *Gannett*, 745 F.2d 774.

significant governmental interest of raising revenue for the self-sufficient, efficient operation of commuter lines.

Gannet did not go away empty handed, however. It won an important concession that became crucial to all future newsrack cases. The MTA is required to adopt regulations that guide its employees in granting licenses and determining licensing terms and that will assure nondiscriminatory treatment.[55]

Only four years later, the first overarching case governing the placement of newsracks was decided by the United States Supreme Court,[56] although the court addressed primarily only one of the issues first raised by Gannett in New York City. After the Cleveland Plain Dealer sought to place newsracks on the sidewalks of Lakewood, Ohio, the city revised an ordinance related to the request. The revision (1) empowered the mayor to grant or deny applications, (2) required the mayor to state reasons for a denial, (3) authored the mayor to impose additional terms and conditions for the city council's issuance of such permits as the mayor deems necessary and reasonable, (4) required approval of the newsrack design by the city's architectural review board, and (5) required the newsrack owner to agree to purchase a $100,000 insurance policy that would indemnify the city against any liability arising from the newsrack. Among other things, the Court ruled that the provisions giving the mayor unlimited discretion to grant or deny permit applications, and to impose additional terms and conditions for the issuance of such permits, violated the Federal Constitution's First Amendment.[57]

One fairly technical legal issue needs to be clarified at this point. Ordinarily, courts will not hear a tort case unless the person who files suit has been injured in some way. The

---

[55] *Gannett*, 745 F.2d 775.

[56] *Lakewood v Plain Dealer Pub. Co.*, 486 US 750 (1988).

[57] *Lakewood*, 486 US 752.

exception to this rule is called a facial challenge. Some statutes threaten individual rights so severely that courts will accept a constitutional challenge to them even if no injury yet has taken place. This is one of those instances. Writes Justice Brennan,

> [w]e have previously identified two major First Amendment risks associated with **unbridled** [emphasis added] licensing schemes: self-censorship by speakers in order to avoid being denied a license to speak; and the difficulty of effectively detecting, reviewing, and correcting content-based censorship 'as applied' without standards by which to measure the licensor's action. It is when statutes threaten these risks to a significant degree that courts must entertain an immediate facial attack on the law.[58]

The majority then placed important and controversial limitations on which laws can be facially challenged when it asserted, "This is not to say that the press or a speaker may challenge as censorship any law involving discretion to which it is subject. The law must have a close enough nexus to expression, or to conduct commonly associated with expression, to pose a real and substantial threat of the identified censorship risks."[59] The core conflict arises from the requirement to determine at what point a law has a sufficient nexus to expression or to conduct commonly associated with expression that it represents a threat to free speech.

The objections raised by Justice White, joined by justices Stevens and O'Connor, in dissent are worth mention. First, the dissent pointed out that this case "does not establish any constitutional right of newspaper publishers to place

---

[58] *Lakewood*, 486 US 759.
[59] *Lakewood*, 486 US 759.

newsracks on municipal property."[60] Although it also does not grant a constitutional right to cities to ban newsracks in public areas, the dissent asserts that "an outright ban on newsracks on city sidewalks would be constitutional, particularly where (as is true here) ample alternative means of 24-hour distribution of newspapers exist."[61] The primary problem the dissent has with the majority, it that the decision grants a special privilege to the placement of newsracks. Public spaces, says White, should be reserved "for use by the public generally, as opposed to the exclusive use of one individual or corporation."[62] Finally, the dissent notes that safety and aesthetics are two legitimate reasons for regulating newsracks.

The primary impact of this case, though, is that any regulations governing the placement of newsracks in public places must not give "unbridled discretion" to the regulators.

Two years later Gannett's objection to newsrack regulations again elicited the attention of a federal appeals court, this time it was the third circuit.[63] After the Port Authority of New York and New Jersey denied Gannett's request to install *USA Today* vending machines throughout Newark Airport, Gannett challenged the denial and the authority revised its rules. Included in the revisions, however, was Rule 10, which stated the following:

> No person shall post, distribute or display at an air terminal a sign, advertisement, circular, or any printed or written matter concerning or referring to commercial activity, except pursuant to a written agreement with the Port Authority

---

[60] *Lakewood*, 486 US 772.

[61] *Lakewood*, 486 US 773.

[62] *Lakewood*, 486 US 781.

[63] *Gannett Satellite Information Network, Inc. v. Berger*, 894 F.2d 61 (3rd Cir. 1990).

specifying the time, place and manner of, and fee or rental for, such activity.[64]

Reflecting on *Lakewood*, Gannet said the rule "amounted to a facially invalid regulatory "scheme" that vested governmental officials with the standardless discretion to censor written expression."[65]

Nevertheless, the federal district court of New Jersey upheld the Port Authority's action as a valid time, place and manner restriction. It said that the airport is a public forum for first amendment purposes, and the Port Authority's denial of permission to Gannett was content-neutral and narrowly tailored to serve significant governmental interests. According to the district court, "The abundance of private newsstands at the airport, moreover, provided Gannett with more than an adequate number of alternative channels of communication."[66]

Again reflecting on *Lakewood*, Gannett did not challenge the district court's time, place, and manner restriction, but focused its appeal to the third circuit on the concept of unbridled discretion, which the third circuit interpreted as an example of what constitutes an overly broad rule. It said that a facial challenge is acceptable when "a governmental official is given complete and unbridled discretion to choose which speakers to favor and which to stifle."[67] To challenge what the court said in essence is rule that is overly broad, Gannett must show "more than a mere possibility that a particular grant of discretion might be used unconstitutionally."[68] It had to show "whether Rule 10 has "a close enough nexus to expression, or to

---

[64] *Gannett*, 894 F.2d 64.
[65] *Gannett*, 894 F.2d 64.
[66] *Gannett*, 894 F.2d 64.
[67] *Gannett*, 894 F.2d 66.
[68] *Gannett*, 894 F.2d 66.

conduct commonly associated with expression, to pose a real and substantial threat" of censorship.'"[69]

Answering its own question, the court says, "We believe that it does," and then it continues:

> There is no question that this regulation directly relates to expression: it confers upon the Port Authority the power to regulate "printed or written matter." Rule 10 gives rise to the very real possibility that officials at the Port Authority, sooner or later, may restrict speech in a way that contravenes the first amendment. We believe that this threat is real and substantial, given the complete absence of any standards guiding the Port Authority.[70]

At bottom, the third circuit says the Port Authority grants itself the same unconstitutional unbridled discretion that the city of Lakewood granted to its mayor. The essential issue, therefore, in developing regulatory schemes for the placement of newsracks in places other than private property is writing rules or standards that are not so broad that they transcend proper time, place, and manner regulations and instead vest overly broad or unbridled discretion in the hands of regulators.

The next case to address newsracks focused not on railroad terminals or sidewalks, but rest areas along interstate highways. In March. 1989, the Florida Department of Transportation told the Sentinel Communications Company, publisher of The Orlando *Sentinel,* that Department of Blind Services had been granted authority to regulate distributors of newspapers in public rest areas along interstate highways.[71] It

---

[69] *Lakewood*, 486 US 759.

[70] *Gannett*, 894 F.2d 67

[71] *Sentinel Communication Co. v. Watts*, 936 F.2d 1189 (11th Cir. 1991).

also said that the company, therefore, was required to apply to T. Jack Bassett, Chief of the Bureau of Business Enterprises for DBS for permission to install newsracks in the rest areas.

Neither the DOT nor the DBS had promulgated written rules or regulations governing Bassett's authority nor were there procedures or standards in place that he was obligated to follow when reviewing requests or applications to install newsracks at rest areas. He also was free to negotiate the amount of the administrative fee on each newspaper sold. In addition, the contract Bassett drew up required the *Sentinel* to maintain a liability insurance policy for the newsracks. Although the insurance provision was present in contracts with other news organizations, Bassett did not require Coke or Pepsi to provide liability insurance.

The fee was intended to compensate the DBS for the cost of administering the agreement and inspecting the vending machines, but Bassett performed no independent cost studies before setting a fee. Instead, he simply conversed with transportation officials in other states who recommended five cents, and he admitted he did not know how much it had cost the DBS to administer *Sentinel's* contract.

At the very first, the court reaffirmed what it said was a well-established First Amendment right to distribute newspapers using newsracks.[72] Some regulations of newsracks, however, have survived a First Amendment attack. Nevertheless, anyone can challenge regulations of newsracks in public places on the ground that they delegate overly broad licensing discretion to a regulator because the United States Supreme Court in essence said in *Lakewood* that some minimal procedures and standards are required to limit discretion.[73] Some neutral criteria must be established, that is, in order to

---

[72] *Sentinel*, 936 F.2d 1195.
[73] *Lakewood*, 486 US 772.

insure that a permit decision regarding newsracks is not based on the content or viewpoint of the speech being considered.

How tightly these standards must be drawn depends upon a forum analysis, and the court ruled that a public rest area is a non-public forum because the practice of allowing some speech activity on interstate property does not amount to the dedication of such property to expressive activities.[74] Since the government did not create rest areas for the purpose of providing a forum for expressive activity; the mere fact that such activity occurs there does not imply that the area thereby becomes a public forum for First Amendment purposes.[75] Consequently, any restriction upon the placement of newsracks in an interstate highway's public rest areas is tested only for reasonableness.[76]

To examine reasonableness, the court pointed out first that, although a licensing fee is permissible, a state may charge no more than the amount needed to cover administrative costs; it may not profit by imposing licensing or permit fees on the exercise of First Amendment rights.[77] The DBS provided no evidence supporting the reasonableness of the administrative fee, which is due in no small part to the absence of any standards, policies, studies, or procedures governing a regulator's discretion in administering the permit scheme. This lack of direction also is reflected in evidence showing that only the newspaper vending machines were being forced to carry liability insurance, while Coke or Pepsi, were exempt from the requirement.

The court, as a result, upheld Sentinel's facial challenge to the constitutionality of Florida's unwritten scheme for permitting placement of newsracks at interstate rest areas. It

---

[74] *Sentinel*, 936 F.2d 1203.

[75] *Sentinel*, 936 F.2d 1204.

[76] *Sentinel*, 936 F.2d 1204.

[77] *Sentinel*, 936 F.2d 1205. See *Cox v. New Hampshire*, 312 U.S. 569, 577 (1941), and *Murdock v. Pennsylvania*, 319 U.S. 105, 113-114 (1943).

said Florida "cannot continue to take an utterly discretionary . . . regulatory approach towards activity that is entitled to first amendment protection; the state agencies in this case must establish some type of written regulatory or statutory scheme with specific criteria to guide the discretion of officials administering it."[78]

This is the fourth case to note that regulations of newracks must meet at least the minimum requirement of being drawn narrowly enough to guarantee that First Amendment protected expression is not discriminated against on the basis of content. This message, however, either is not eagerly accepted by regulators or not easily implemented by governments.

Cincinnati provides the local for the fifth recent case to focus on newsrack regulations.[79] Once again the United States Supreme Court weighed in. The Discovery Network provided adult educational, recreational, and social programs to residents in the Cincinnati area. It advertises these programs in a free magazine that it publishes nine times a year. Although the magazine consist primarily of promotional material pertaining to Discovery's courses, it also includes information about current events of general interest.

Harmon Publishing publishes a magazine that advertises real estate for sale at various locations throughout the United States. It contains listings and photographs of available residential properties in the greater Cincinnati area, and also includes information about interest rates, market trends, and other real estate matters. In March 1990, the city's director of public works notified Discovery and Harmon that their permits to use newsracks on public property was revoked and ordered them removed.

The United States Supreme Court agreed with both the district and appeals court that the test for evaluating the city's

---

[78] *Sentinel*, 936 F.2d 1207.
[79] *Cincinnati v. Discovery Network, Inc.*, 570 U.S. 410 (1993).

regulation was whether the city's announced goal or purpose for regulating the newsracks--safety and aesthesis--is a "reasonable fit" with the means used--in this case removal--to achieve that goal.[80]

The Court held that, in fact, the city had not established a reasonable fit for several reasons. First, the ordinance on which the city relied had been enacted, long before any concern about newsracks developed, for the apparent purpose of preventing the kind of visual blight caused by littering. Second, the city failure to address its recently developed concern about newsracks by taking the approach of regulating their size, shape, appearance, or number indicates that it has not carefully calculated the costs and benefits associated with the burden on speech imposed by its prohibition. Third, the prohibition required the removal of only a small portion--62 out of about 1,500 to 2,000--of the newsracks in the city.[81]

The Court also said the city's ban was an impermissible means of responding to the city's legitimate interests in safety and esthetics. First, the ban placed too much importance on the distinction between commercial speech and noncommercial speech. Second, such a distinction bore no relationship to the particular interests asserted (safety and aesthetics). Third, the ban was not a content-neutral restriction on the time, place, or manner of engaging in protected speech because the very basis for the regulation was the difference in content between ordinary newspapers and commercial speech, and because rather than merely limiting the number of newsracks, the city had limited to zero the number of newsracks distributing commercial publications.[82]

Two important considerations were given attention by the Court. Safety and aesthetics are legitimate interests that

---

[80] *Board of Trustees of State University of N. Y. v. Fox*, 492 U.S. 469 (1989).
[81] *Cincinnati, 570 US 415.*
[82] *Cincinnati, 570 US 429.*

support governmental regulations of newsracks as long as they are content-neutral. In addition, commercial publications have the same rights regarding the limitations newsrack regulations as do non-commercial publications.

The regulations of newsracks placed on sidewalks once again attracted the attention of an appeals court. Just before the City of Coral Gables, Florida, adopted a newsrack ordinance in March of 1992, Gold Coast Publications, Inc. began publishing !Exito! a tabloid-style, weekly Spanish-language newspaper directed at young, educated Hispanic professionals. Since the new tabloid did not conform to some aspects of the ordinance, Gold Coast filed suit claiming parts of it were unconstitutional.[83] Among the requirements of the ordinance are these: the newsracks were obligated to have gloss brown pedestals, gloss beige sides and door, and gloss brown coin boxes; card holders or advertisements on the racks were prohibited; they must be placed parallel to the curb between eighteen and twenty-four inches from the edge of the curb or parallel to a building not more than six inches from the building's wall, and the name of the newspaper could be displayed on the sides, front, and back of the newsrack as long as the lettering was no larger than 1-3/4 inches in height and centered at fifteen inches from the top of the cabinet.[84] !Exito!, which means success or hit in Spanish, was distributed free solely through newsracks. To attract readers, the published provided newsracks painted deep purple and prominently displayed the !Exito! logo in lime green, bright orange, or hot pink.

Gold Cost claimed the location restrictions were overbroad and not rationally related to health, safety, and welfare; the ordinance did not subject other vending machines or fixtures, such as trash receptacles, to the uniform color and

---

[83] *Gold Coast Publications v. Corrigan*, 42 F.3d 1336 (11th Cir. 1994).
[84] *Gold Coast* 42 F.3d 1336.

lettering requirements; and the requirement of uniform color and the limitation on the size of lettering were not valid time, place, or manner restrictions.

Addressing first the question of what type of forum is the area where the racks were placed, the court ruled that the locations are unambiguously a traditional public forum since they are clearly in the public rights-of-way. Since government's ability to limit expression in a public forum is "sharply circumscribed,"[85] a content-neutral limitation on the time, place, or manner of expression must be narrowly tailored to serve a significant government interest and must provide ample alternative channels of communication.

Regarding the first prong of the time, place, or manner test, the city contended that ordinance is narrowly tailored to support safety and aesthetic interests. The test for narrowly tailored is that the ordinance be "not substantially broader than necessary." [86] Thus, the eleventh circuit agreed with the district court ruling that evidence linking the regulation to pedestrian and vehicular safety interests is substantiated. It also said the uniform color and size of lettering requirements are narrowly tailored to achieve the city's aesthetic objectives. To the argument that other fixtures in the business district, such as awnings and trash receptacles, do not have to meet the color and lettering restrictions, the court said simply that the city can enact partial solutions to further its aesthetic interests; it is not required to have a comprehensive plan to improve aesthetics.[87]

In addition, the court said that, because ample alternative channels for communication are available, the disputed color and lettering regulations satisfy the second prong of the time, place, or manner test and so constitute valid restrictions. Although the limitations on regulations of

---

[85] *Perry Educ. Ass'n*, 460 U.S. at 45.
[86] *Gold Coast* 42 F.3d 1345.
[87] *Gold Coast* 42 F.3d 1347.

expression in the public fora are more stringent than those for expression in non-public fora, the city was able to conform to the limits primarily through the use of very specific descriptions and carefully drafted language. Unlike the regulations that offered unbridled discretion to a regulator, the ordinances of Coral Gables were explicit and coherent. It appears that ten years after the first modern federal court decision on newsracks, at least some governments have learned how to draw up regulations that pass constitutional muster.

A return to airports as a venue for regulated newsracks took place in 1997.[88] When Harlan L. Jacobsen, publisher of *Solo RFD*, a monthly newspaper providing services and advice to single persons, tired to install newsracks in the Rapid City, South Dakota, airport, William Bacon, the airport administrator for the city, told him the papers would have to be sold through the gift shop. Jacobsen then won from the district court an injunction stopping the airport from keeping out his newsracks. The eighth circuit agreed with the district court that the airport is not a public forum, and so the newsrack policy need be only reasonable, as long as it is not an effort to suppress a speaker's activity based on a speaker's content.

Although the city claimed the policy supported its important interests in airport maintenance, safety, security, operational efficiency, aesthetics, and revenue (which are legitimate government interests) the circuit court accepted only one of reasons supporting these interests. To the city's claim that newsracks interfere with airport maintenance, the court responded that the only support was vague hearsay testimony of complaints by cleaning crews. The court said the city presented no evidence of injury to support its worry that newsracks are unstable or top heavy. When city witnesses testified that newsracks would be used to conceal a bomb, the court called the testimony speculative and characterized it as simply a

---

[88] *Jacobsen v City of Rapid City*, 128 F.3d 660 (8th Cir. 1997).

pretext because the terminal has many other places where a bomb could be hidden. Although the city claimed newsracks would affect negatively airport operations, the court found that, even in high-traffic areas, newsracks are sufficiently removed from pedestrian traffic to avoid obstructing or impeding travelers. Finally, to the city's assertion that newsracks detract from airport decor, the court found that the appearance of Jacobsen's newsracks was not incompatible. It also noted that, although airport decor may be regulated, it rarely, if ever, would justify a total ban on newsracks.[89]

Nevertheless, the court did agree with the city that "a certain amount of commercial retail activity is consistent with the intended uses of an airport terminal, and making newspapers reasonably available to air travelers is a compatible commercial activity."[90] It pointed out that the presence of newsracks would decrease revenues for the gift shop, "making its exclusive contract [with the shop] less valuable. That in turn will reduce the City's leverage in bargaining for terms such as minimum annual concession fees and pro rata utility charges."[91]

Furthermore, the district court erred, said the eighth circuit, when it ruled the city was not permitted to make a profit from the sale of the newspapers. It said that, when the city acts as sovereign, it may not make a profit, but when it acts as a proprietor, then "it is presumptively reasonable for the manager of a small airport to conclude that granting one gift shop concessionaire the exclusive right to sell consumer products in the terminal will both maximize that type of leasing revenues and minimize leasing costs by eliminating the need to negotiate with many different types of vendors."[92] Moreover, the court noted, "Jacobsen presented no evidence at trial of the impact that selling *Solo RFD* in the gift shop would have on its sales

---

[89] *Jacobsen*, 128 F.3d 662.
[90] *Jacobsen*, 128 F.3d 663.
[91] *Jacobsen*, 128 F.3d 662.
[92] *Jacobsen*, 128 F.3d 664.

and circulation in the Airport terminal."[93]   Consequently, the eighth circuit said the,"[t]he district court's finding that the gift shop is not a 'viable alternative channel[] for the sale of Jacobsen's newspapers' was speculation, unsupported by the evidence."[94]

Therefore, the court ruled, "Until Jacobsen comes forward with concrete evidence that the City's ... policy ... either is intended to discriminate or unreasonably fails to provide *Solo RFD* a viable means of airport distribution"[95] the City's proprietary revenue interest in operating the airport for the benefit of air travelers justifies its total ban on newsracks. In other words, as long as the city does not use the excuse of newracks as a way to garner revenue, it can regulate them in such a way that it   This is the same message the second circuit sent Gannett when it tried to block regulations of newsracks in a railroad station. If the government is operating a business, then it can impose regulations that result in a profit for the taxpayers.

It appears that airport regulations of newsracks constitute the most common reason for the mass media to claim constitutional violations. The Atlanta *Journal-Constitution* challenged in federal court the city of Atlanta's 1996 plan to replace privately-owned racks with city-owned newsracks at Hartsfield Atlanta International Airport.[96]   The plan had three other important parts. "The newsracks were part of an airport promotion in conjunction with the 1996 Olympic Games and Coca-Cola was to play a major role in the Olympic promotion. Accordingly, the newsracks were to display advertisements for Coca-Cola,"[97] but only a limited size of the paper's own logo. In addition newspapers were required to pay $ 20 per month

---

[93] *Jacobsen*, 128 F.3d 663.

[94] *Jacobsen*, 128 F.3d 664.

[95] *Jacobsen*, 128 F.3d 665.

[96] *Atlanta Journal and Constitution v. The City of Atlanta Department of Aviation*, 107 F. Supp. 2d 1375 (N.D.Ga. 2000).

[97] *Atlanta Journal and Constitution*, 107 F.Supp. 1377.

rental fee for each newsrack. Third, the decision to grant a permit for a newsrack would be based on a "desire" to have diversity of viewpoints in the airport and the department could cancel a permit on thirty days notice.[98]

In contrast to the second circuit, the eleventh circuit, basing its opinion on a Pennsylvania case, ruled that an airport is a non-public forum. Nevertheless, restrictions on speech are permissible in a non-public forum, said the court, so long as they are viewpoint-neutral and reasonable. Since "no aspect of selling newspaper through newsracks is inherently inconsistent with facilitating air travel," said the court, the government must show a reason for placing restrictions on the racks.[99] The Atlanta *Journal-Constitution* proffered four reasons asserting that the restrictions are unreasonable and so violate the First Amendment.

The first is the number and placement of the racks. Because "in formulating the 1996 plan the city did not consider the reasons it now offers to justify the number and placement of the boxes,"[100] the court said it cannot rule that the 1996 plan is reasonable. Indeed, it appears pretextual. Nor can the court say it is unreasonable, however, because "the number and placement of the newsracks appears to be in keeping with historical locations (in the terminal), and actually expanded the number of newsracks available to the AJC from eighteen to about thirty."[101]

The newspaper's objections to the requirement that restricted the size of their own logos and while demanding the newsracks feature large advertisements for Coca-Cola was upheld. The court said this requirement is unconstitutional "because the distinction based on speaker identity is

---

[98] *Atlanta Journal and Constitution*, 107 F.Supp. 1378.

[99] *Atlanta Journal and Constitution*, 107 F.Supp. 1379.

[100] *Atlanta Journal and Constitution*, 107 F.Supp. 1380.

[101] *Atlanta Journal and Constitution*, 107 F.Supp. 1379.

unreasonable."[102]   The city's gratitude for Coca-Cola's underwriting its cultural programs, said the court, is not a sufficient reason to compel the newspapers "to associate their publications with Coca-Cola products ... through newsracks."[103]

Although a licensing fee is permissible in a non-public forum, the city may charge no more than the amount needed to cover administrative costs. Writes the court, "The government may not profit by imposing licensing or permit fees on the exercise of first amendment rights, and is prohibited from raising revenue under the guise of defraying its administrative costs."[104]   Since no evidence was produced to show the 1996 plan's $20 per month fee was tied solely to administrative costs, the court ruled the fee unconstitutional. This ruling contrasts sharply with the second circuit, which said making a profit off newsracks serves "the government interest of effective and efficient air travel for the public."[105]

What the court called "unbridled discretion"[106] constituted the strongest reason, however, for declaring unconstitutional the newsrack regulation scheme. The essential problem with the regulation, said the court, is that "it vests unbridled discretion in airport personnel who may choose which publications are granted access to the city-owned newsracks."[107] This discretion includes not only determining what publications are displayed on the sole basis of "diversity,"[108] but also the "ability to cancel a permit without offering any kind of reason at all."[109]   Writes the court, "[e]ven if space were allocated

---

[102] *Atlanta Journal and Constitution*, 107 F.Supp. 1380.
[103] *Atlanta Journal and Constitution*, 107 F.Supp. 1380.
[104] *Atlanta Journal and Constitution*, 107 F.Supp. 1381.
[105] *Atlanta Journal and Constitution*, 107 F.Supp. 1381.
[106] *Atlanta Journal and Constitution*, 107 F.Supp. 1382.
[107] *Atlanta Journal and Constitution*, 107 F.Supp. 1382.
[108] *Atlanta Journal and Constitution*, 107 F.Supp. 1383.
[109] *Atlanta Journal and Constitution*, 107 F.Supp. 1383.

neutrally in the first instance, the mere existence of the power to exclude a publication for no reason at all could "intimidate . . . parties into censoring their own speech."[110]

As a result, the court permanently enjoined the city of Atlanta Department of Aviation from enacting any newsrack plat at Hartsfield Atlanta International Airport which featured the following characteristics:[111] (1) requires the display of advertisements for other products, (2) requires a fee not tied to the cost of administering the newsracks, (3) vests unbridled discretion in an authority who selects which publications may place newsracks at the airport or who determines which publications may continue to maintain a rack.

This case takes the law full circle. Nearly two decades after the second circuit required the MTA to adopt regulations that guide its employees in granting licenses and determining licensing terms and that will assure nondiscriminatory treatment, the eleventh circuit also said vesting unbridled authority in a regulator is unconstitutional.

Summary of newsrack regulations

The right to distribute newspapers using newsracks clearly is granted by the First Amendment.[112] This protection,

---

[110] *Atlanta Journal and Constitution*, 107 F.Supp. 1383, quoting *Lakewood* 486 U.S. 757.

[111] *Atlanta Journal and Constitution*, 107 F.Supp. 1384.

[112] *See e.g., Gannett Satellite Information Network, Inc. v. Berger*, 716 F.Supp. 140, 146 (N.J. 1989); *Gannett Satellite Information Network, Inc. v. Metropolitan Transportation Authority*, 745 F.2d 767, 772 (2nd Cir. 1984); *Miami Herald Publishing Company v. City of Hallandale*, 734 F.2d 666, 673 (11th Cir. 1984); *Chicago Newspaper Publishers Ass'n v. City of Wheaton*, 697 F. Supp. 1464, 1466 (N.D. Ill. 1988); *Providence Journal Co. v. City of Newport*, 665 F. Supp. 107, 110 (D.R.I. 1987); *Southern New Jersey Newspapers v. New Jersey Department of Transportation*, 542 F. Supp. 173, 183 (D.N.J. 1982); *Passaic Daily News v. City of Clifton*, 200 N.J. Super. 468, 473, 491 A.2d 808, 11 Media L. Rep. 1962 (Law Div. 1985). *But see, City of Lakewood v. Plain Dealer [*147] Pub. Co.*, 486 U.S. 750, 108 S. Ct. [**19] 2138, 2155, 100 L. Ed. 2d 771 (White, J, dissenting).

however, is limited. The first limit to be investigated is simply the place where a newsrack is located. These locations are analyzed by the courts according to their function as a forum for speech. For purposes of all modes of free speech analysis, including newsracks, the Supreme Court identified (in a case originating from a high school free-speech controversy) three types of fora: the traditional public forum, the limited or designated public forum, and the non-public forum.[113] A traditional public forum is a place "which by long tradition or by government fiat has been devoted to assembly and debate," such as a street or park.[114]

The government creates a limited public forum when it opens its property "'for indiscriminate use by the general public,' or by some segment of the public."[115] The government may also designate a forum for a limited purpose, such as use by certain speakers or the discussion of specific topics.[116] (university meeting places are designated public forum for use by student groups). Moreover, courts do not presume the government passively has converted a nonpublic forum into a limited public forum unless, "by policy or by practice,"[117] the government has demonstrated a clear intent to do so.[118] Finally, forum analysis may focus on whether a particular location is compatible with expressive activity.[119]

In either a traditional or a limited public forum, government may impose content-based restrictions on speech only if they are necessary to serve a compelling state interest

---

[113] *Perry Educ. Ass'n v. Perry Local Educators' Ass'n,* 460 U.S. 37, 45, (1983).

[114] Perry, 460 U.S. at 45.

[115] *Hazelwood,* 108 S. Ct. at 568 (quoting *Perry,* 460 U.S. at 47).

[116] *Cornelius v. NAACP Legal Defense & Educ. Fund, Inc.,* 473 U.S. 788, 802, (1985); *Perry,* 460 U.S. at 45-46 & n. 7; *see also Widmar v. Vincent,* 454 U.S. 263 (1981).

[117] *Perry,* 460 U.S. at 47

[118] *Cornelius,* 473 U.S. at 802.

[119] *Kincaid,* 236 F.3d at 349.

and are narrowly tailored to accomplish that interest.[120] Government also may enforce time, place, and manner regulations if they are content-neutral, are narrowly tailored to serve a significant government interest, and leave open ample alternative channels of communication." *Perry, supra,* at 45 In a nonpublic forum, however, restrictions on speech need be only "reasonable and not an effort to suppress expression merely because public officials oppose the speaker's view."[121]

The United States Supreme Court came up with a test for determining whether regulations of newsracks are content based when it ruled that some minimal procedures and standards are required to limit the discretion of a regulator. Some neutral criteria must be established in a newsrack policy, that is, in order to insure that a decision by a regulator is not based on the content or viewpoint of the speech being considered.[122]

A time, place and manner test that the United States Supreme Court said was constitutionally acceptable for evaluating newsrack regulations was considering whether a regulation reasonably fit any avowed safety and aesthetic concerns.[123] which ruled that government had the burden of establishing a reasonable fit between the legislature's ends and the means chosen to accomplish those ends.

Regarding the narrowly tailored prong of the time, place, or manner test, the rubric is a requirement that a newsrack regulation be "not substantially broader than necessary." This is not as burdensome as the test the media usually prefer, that the restriction must be "no greater than

---

[120] *Cornelius,* 473 U.S. at 800; *Perry,* 460 U.S. at 45; *Carey v. Brown,* 447 U.S. 455, 461 (1981).

[121] *Perry,* 460 U.S. at 46; *see also Cornelius,* 473 U.S. at 800.

[122] *Lakewood,* 486 U.S. at 772.

[123] *Cincinnati v. Discovery Network, Inc.,* 570 U.S. 410, 414 (1993), making reference to Board of Trustees of State University of N. Y. v. Fox, 492 U.S. 469,(1989).

necessary" or no "broader than necessary" to fulfill a government interest in safety or aesthetics.[124] The Supreme Court, however, expressly rejected the "less-restrictive-alternative analysis" for time, place, or manner regulations.[125] Instead, the Court adopted a "not substantially broader than necessary" standard to evaluate whether a regulation is narrowly tailored.[126]

The analysis is a bit more complex than simply choosing one of these two standards. Although the United States Supreme Court as rejected the "least-restrictive-means" test for judging time, place, and manner restrictions on speech, it also has rejected what it called a "mere rational-basis" review. A regulation need not be "absolutely the least severe that will achieve the desired end,"[127] but if there are numerous and obvious less-burdensome alternatives to restrictions on speech, then the Court said these alternative represent a relevant consideration in determining whether the "fit" between ends and means is reasonable.[128]

In summary, the reasonable-fit standard requires that, regulations of newsracks must show a fit between governments avowed goals--such as safety or aesthetics--and the means chosen to accomplish those ends; such a fit (1) must be reasonable, but not necessarily perfect, (2) must represent not necessarily the single best disposition, but one whose scope is in proportion to the interest served, and (3) must employ not necessarily the least restrictive means, but a means narrowly tailored to achieve the desired objective; although a regulation

---

[124] Gold Coast, 798 F. Supp. at 1571.

[125] *Ward v. Rock Against Racism*, 491 U.S. 781, 797-800, (1989) (upholding an ordinance limiting the volume of music at concerts in Central Park's Naumberg Acoustic Bandshell) (citing *Regan v. Time, Inc.*, 468 U.S. 641, 657 (1984) (White, J.)).

[126] *Ward*, 491 U.S. at 800.

[127] *Fox*, 492 U.S. at 480.

[128] *Cincinnati v. Discovery Network, Inc.*, 570 U.S. 410, 416 (1993)

need not be absolutely the least severe that will achieve the desired end, the fact that there are numerous and obvious less-burdensome alternatives to the restriction is a relevant consideration in determining whether the fit between ends and means is reasonable. Furthermore, the government goal must be substantial, and the cost must be carefully calculated

Much of the controversy over newracks focuses on airports. Most, but not all, courts have ruled that an airport is not a public forum for First Amendment purposes, and so a newsrack regulation need be only reasonable, as long as it is not an effort to suppress a speaker's activity based on a speaker's content. Jacobsen Since "no aspect of selling newspaper through newsracks is inherently inconsistent with facilitating air travel," said one court, the government must show a reason for placing restrictions on the racks.

The controversy over reasonableness has focused on the profit motive. If the government is acting in its role as a sovereign when regulating newsracks, then a licensing fee is a permissible as a reasonable time, place, or manner regulation only if it does not make a profit. It may charge what it needs to cover administrative coasts, but it may not profit by imposing licensing or permit fees on the exercise of First Amendment rights. If the government takes on the role of a proprietor, however, and in essence becomes a business, then it is entitled to earn a profit as is any business. Thus, if the government runs an airport, then it can promulgate newsrack regulations that result in a profit. If the government simply is regulating newsracks in a private airport, however, then it may not pass an ordinance that results in what amounts to a profit.

Chapter 7

Access to Government: Open Records and Open Meetings

By Robert D. Richards

Introduction

On April 25, 1682, William Penn set forth the frame of government for Pennsylvania, stating "Let men be good, and the government cannot be bad; if it be ill, they will cure it."[1] Notwithstanding the gender bias of his comment, Penn recognized almost three-and-a-quarter centuries ago the importance of ensuring that good people be placed in government service. For the electorate to ensure that the appropriate individuals are in place--and continue to operate with integrity--citizens need ways to find out what government is doing. Starting with the basic premise that government should operate for the people of the state and be accessible to them, the Pennsylvania General Assembly enacted two measures designed to open the government to the public. The first law, enacted in the late fifties and used to provide access to documents -- records of government agencies -- for more than

---

[1] William Penn, "The Frame of the Government [of Pennsylvania], and the Laws Agreed Upon in England, in Neil H. Cogan, *Contexts of the Constitution*, p. 8 (New York: Foundation Press, 1999).

four decades is popularly referred to as the Right-to-Know Act.[2] This measure was dramatically altered in 2002, providing greater access to information than ever contemplated under the old law. The second major tool is the Pennsylvania Sunshine Act,[3] known formerly as the Open Meeting Law. The Act was first passed in 1974 and subsequently overhauled into a new version that took effect in 1987.

Despite these laws and their refinements, much of the enforcement and interpretation has fallen into the hands of the courts. In Pennsylvania, that process begins, most times, in the courts of common pleas of the appropriate judicial district, except in the case of a "Sunshine Act" dispute against a state agency. In such instances, the case begins in the Commonwealth Court, the judicial organ that ordinarily handles appeals of cases where a state or local government body is a party.

The case illustrations throughout this chapter serve to add flesh to the skeletal structure the legislative enactments already provide. Rest assured, however, that Pennsylvania courts will continue to grapple with the interpretation of these important acts.

Right-to-Know Act

After several years of legislative wrangling, a new open records law has emerged in the state. Several interested parties, including the Pennsylvania Newspaper Association, labored tirelessly over the past several years to revise – if not completely scrap -- the vastly outdated 1957 statute. The compromise bill that was signed into law on June 29, 2002 by Governor Mark Schweiker (and became effective on December 26, 2002) gave none of the principal actors exactly what they wanted but did nudge the state forward through the nearly half-

---

[2] 65 Pa. C.S.A. § 66.1 et. seq. (2002)
[33] 65 Pa. C.S.A. § 701 et. seq. (2000).

century of technological and informational innovations that had occurred since the old law went into effect.

While the passage of the new Act may be cause for quiet celebration, Pennsylvania still lags behind other states in the allowing its citizens the kind of unbridled access that results in an informed citizenry.

Some of the highlights of the new Act include an expanded definition of what constitutes an "agency" under the law. The main changes include the addition of the State System of Higher Education and offices within the executive branch. The definition reads as follows:

> Any office, department, board or commission of the executive branch of the Commonwealth, any political subdivision of the Commonwealth, the Pennsylvania Turnpike Commission, the state system of higher education or any State or municipal authority or similar organization created by or pursuant to a statute which declares in substance that such organization performs or has for its purpose the performance of an essential governmental function.

While the definition of "agency" is expansive -- it includes all counties and municipalities throughout Pennsylvania and supercedes any conflicting home rule charters[4] -- state-related universities, such as Penn State and Temple, have been ruled exempt.[5] Consequently, budgetary and salary information from these institutions need not be made

---

[4] Moak v. Philadelphia Newspaper, Inc., 336 A. 2d 920 (Pa. Commw. Ct. 1975).

[5] Roy v. Pennsylvania State University, 568 A. 2d 751 (Pa. Commw. Ct. 1990) ; Mooney v. Board of Trustees of Temple University of the Commonwealth System of Higher Education, 292 A. 2d 395 (Pa. 1972).

public despite the fact that each institution receives some state funding.

The Commonwealth Court also has ruled that an agency performing an essential governmental function is not exempt from the Act simply because it is not specifically mentioned in the statute.[6] It is not sufficient, however, that an organization is labeled a "Commonwealth agency" under another statute.[7] Oddly, though, the General Assembly as well as the Pennsylvania courts remain outside the definition of agency.

The new law is more specific with respect to the procedure for obtaining access. The general rule is as follows:

> Unless otherwise provided by law, a public record shall be accessible for inspection and duplication by a requester in accordance with this act. A public record shall be provided to a requester in the medium requested if the public record exists in that medium; otherwise, it shall be provided in the medium in which it exists. Public records shall be available for access during the regular business hours of an agency. Nothing in this act shall provide for access to a record which is not a public record.

Throughout the history of the open record laws in Pennsylvania, the definition of "public record"[8] has resulted in numerous trips to the courts for interpretation. In fact, most of the litigation over open records revolves around this definition. It is stated as follows in the statute:

---

[6] A.R. Building Company v. Pennsylvania Housing Finance Agency, 500 A. 2d 943 (Pa. Commw. Ct. 1985).

[7] Safety, Agric., Villages & Env't, Inc. v. Del. Valley Reg'l Planning Commn., 819 A.2d 1235 (Pa. Commw. 2003).

[8] 65 Pa. C.S.A. § 66.1.

Any account, voucher or contract dealing with the receipt or disbursement of funds by an agency or its acquisition, use or disposal of services or of supplies, materials, equipment or other property and any minute, order or decision by an agency fixing the personal or property rights, privileges, immunities, duties or obligations of any person or group of persons:

This definition, however, contains a limiting proviso:

Provided, that the term "public records" shall not mean any report, communication or other paper, the publication of which would disclose the institution, progress or result of an investigation undertaken by an agency in the performance of its official duties, except those reports filed by agencies pertaining to safety and health in industrial plants; it shall not include any record, document, material, exhibit, pleading, report, memorandum or other paper, access to or the publication of which is prohibited, restricted or forbidden by statute law or order or decree of court, or which would operate to the prejudice or impairment of a person's reputation or personal security, or which would result in the loss by the Commonwealth or any of its political subdivisions or commissions or State or municipal authorities of Federal funds, excepting therefrom however the record of any conviction for any criminal act.

The application of this definition in numerous cases provides some guidance as to which specific records are public.

Employment Records

One area in which litigation has been particularly heavy involves records related to employment issues. The salaries of government employees are generally available, but litigation of other personnel matters has yielded mixed results. Consider, for example, when a state police officer who was removed from duty sought access to his personnel file. The court ruled he was entitled to inspect it. The officer's removal from duty was part of a "decision," and that decision did indeed "establish, alter, abolish or deny rights, privileges, immunities, duties or obligations as required by the Act."[9] Yet, the previous year the same court found that a public school teacher had no right of access to her personnel file.[10] The court there found that under the Act, "[a] decision 'fixing' the rights or duties of a person is not the same thing as a gathering of information, notations, and evaluations that may or may not be utilized at some future time to reach a decision that would fix rights or duties."[11]

Presumably, courts find certain employment information, such as disciplinary rulings, private. In one such case of a police officer who was suspended from duty, the court refused to force the city to hand over a transcript of the closed proceeding which resulted in the disciplinary action.[12] Nonetheless, a citizen who can glean the otherwise confidential information from multiple sets of documents is free to do so. Thus, matching attendance records of employees with salary records has been an effective tool in discovering such information (e.g., an unexplained void in payroll). The Commonwealth Court, for example, has found that attendance records of school district employees are public records.[13]

---

[9] Lamolinara v. Barger, 373 A. 2d 788, 790 (Pa. Commw. Ct. 1977).

[10] West Shore School District v. Homick, 353 A. 2d 93 (Pa. Commw. Ct. 1976).

[11] Id. at 95.

[12] Mellin v. City of Allentown, 430 A. 2d 1048 (Pa. Commw. Ct. 1981).

[13] Kanzelmeyer v. Eger, 329 A. 2d 307 (Pa. Commw. Ct. 1974).

When the records contain too much confidential information -- names, addresses, phone numbers and social security numbers -- courts can prohibit disclosure on the grounds of personal security. A labor union sought the payroll records of a contractor that was doing roofing work for the North Hills School District. The union was attempting to see if the contractor -- a non-union company (and by extension the school district) -- was paying workers in accordance with the Prevailing Wage Act. The court found that "after balancing this weak public interest in the disclosure of the information and the unproven ability of the release of the requested information to assist in the enforcement of the prevailing wage laws against the individual's right to privacy and personal security," the information should not be released.[14]

Public Funds

Documents relating to the expediture of public funds is another high traffic area for the courts. The Act, itself, deals specifically with the receipt and disbursement of funds and makes certain records generally available. Nonetheless, countless hours of litigation have resulted in expanded availability of these records. One case helped unveil the sensitive area of settlement agreements involving public funds. Often in such lawsuits, the parties agree to keep the terms of the settlement confidential. When Lower Saucon Township reached an out-of-court settlement with a party who had alleged his civil rights were violated by the township's police officers, the court found, "[b]ecause it obligates the township to disburse public funds to satisfy an obligation, the settlement agreement is a public record and subject to public inspection and copying."[15]

---

[14] Sapp Roofing Co., Inc., v. Sheet Metal Workers' Int'l Assoc., 713 A.2d 627, 630 (Pa. 1998).
[15] Morning Call, Inc. v. Lower Saucon Township, 627 A. 2d 297, 300 (1993).

The result was the same for the U.G.I. Utilities, Inc. when it was involved in a dispute with the Allentown Housing Authority. The *Morning Call* newspaper tried to obtain copies of the settlement agreement between the parties, but the Housing Authority reported to the newspaper that it could not release an unredacted copy of the release because U.G.I. Utilities would not agree to waive the confidentiality provision. Commonwealth Court affirmed the trial judge's decision that the agreement is a public record, subject to access, because although a private insurance carrier -- rather than the agency itself -- paid out the claim, "laundering funds through an insurance carrier did not change their essentially public character."[16] Moreover, Commonwealth Court recently ruled that there is no basis for the proposition that "absent court order, decisional law or statutory law to the contrary, a confidentiality clause in a settlement agreement removes the settlement agreement from public disclosure or public scrutiny."[17]

In similar fashion, when a reporter for *The Scranton Times* asked to see cancelled checks on the Carbondale Township's Road Account and Payroll Account, township officials refused his request. The court ruled, however, that "[t]he Act provides that every public record shall be open for examination and inspection. The cancelled checks here are, without question, accounts dealing with the disbursement of funds, a category of documents within the Act's definition of public records."[18] In fact, the court ordered the township to authorize its bank to produce copies of the cancelled checks if the township did not have actual possession of them. The court held in a later case that a citizen was entitled to inspect the

---

[16] Morning Call, Inc. v. Housing Auth. of City of Allentown, 769 A.2d 1246, 1249 (Pa. Commw. Ct. 2001).

[17] Cogan v. Commonwealth, 814 A.2d 825, 828 (Pa. Commw. 2003).

[18] Carbondale Township v. Murray, 440 A. 2d 1273, 1274 (Pa. Commw. Ct. 1982).

Pennsylvania Department of Treasury's list of unclaimed and uncashed checks.[19]

But compare what happens when a newspaper seeks copies of delinquent tax lists for businesses that had not paid wage and business taxes to the municipality. *The Scranton Times* attempted to obtain this type of document from the tax office, but found no such list existed. Consequently, it sought the right to examine individual tax files to compile its own list. The trial court agreed, prompting the tax office to file an appeal, arguing "the trial court's decision was erroneous because it did not have nor was it required to make a list from existing tax records."[20] On appeal, the Commonwealth Court reversed the trial court's decision, saying not only should the tax office not have to compile a list, but also it is strictly forbidden from allowing information from the files to be divulged under the Local Tax Enabling Act.[21] This case illustrates the problem that arises when different statutes govern the release of information, such as the case with police matter below.

Police Matters

Anyone interested in obtaining police information should consult not only the Right-to-Know Act but also the Criminal History Record Information Act (CHRI Act), as well as the common law.[22] These acts need to be read in conjunction with each other.[23] The CHRI Act governs the type of material that must be recorded by the police and how much of it can be made public. Nonetheless, if the CHRI Act does not

---

[19] Anders v. Commonwealth Department of Treasury, 585 A. 2d 568 (Pa. Commw. Ct. 1991).

[20] Scranton Times v. Scranton Single Tax Office, 736 A.2d 711, 712 (Pa Commw. Ct. 1999)

[21] Id. at 714.

[22] 18 Pa. C.S. A. § 9101 et seq.

[23] Lebanon News Publishing Co. v. City of Lebanon, 541 A. 2d 266 (Pa. Commw. Ct. 1982).

specifically require disclosure of particular information, the Right-to-Know Act may provide another avenue of recourse. For example, when reporters for the *Lebanon Daily News* wanted access to a police blotter, a chronological listing of arrests made, they were denied access by the police. Commonwealth Court ruled that dissemination of police blotters to the public was not required under the CHRI Act, but because that Act did classify police logs as "public records," they should be available under the Right-to-Know Act.[24] Note, however, that the definition of police blotter often varies from department to department.

Consequently, obtaining police information often proves to be a difficult task for reporters and other citizens. A common law right of access may be claimed with respect to warrants and supporting affidavits. When the *Morning Call* newspaper wanted to inspect and copy affidavits of probable cause supporting an arrest warrant, the district magistrate denied the paper's request. When the case was ultimately decided, the Pennsylvania Supreme Court relied upon U.S. Supreme Court recognition of a First Amendment right of access to the criminal process. In attaching a presumption of openness to probable cause affidavits, the Pennsylvania Supreme Court wrote:

> Specifically, from a policy standpoint, public inspection of arrest warrant affidavits would serve to discourage perjury in such affidavits, would enhance the performance of police and prosecutors by encouraging them to establish sufficient cause before an affidavit is filed, would act as a public check on discretion of issuing authorities thus discouraging erroneous decisions and decisions based on partiality, and

---

[24] Id. at 268.

would promote a public perception of fairness in the arrest warrant process.[25]

Similarly, search warrants that have been executed are presumptively open under the same rationale.[26] Note, however, that judges may seal the affidavits until the arraignment if the commonwealth makes a sufficient showing.[27]

Criminal investigation reports present a different result. The Commonwealth Court has upheld a police department's refusal to allow access by an assault victim to the on-going investigation file in her case. The Court relied on the part of the "public record" definition which exempts "any report, communication or other paper the publication of which would disclose the institution, progress or result of an investigation undertaken by an agency in the performance of its official duties."[28] Ordinarily, police reports from investigations, even inactive ones, are not public records.[29]

Finally, the news media often attempt to obtain audio tape recordings of telephone calls to emergency response centers. In Pennsylvania, such calls are not considered public records because they "are neither minutes, orders, or decisions fixing rights or duties, nor bear a sufficient association with such forms of agency determinations to require their disclosure under the provisions of the Act."[30]

Reports and Memoranda

When the patients of a state psychiatric hospital sought access to the accreditor's evaluation report on the hospital, they

---

[25] Commonwealth v. Fenstermaker, 530 A.2d 414, 418 (Pa. 1987).

[26] P.G. Publishing Co. v. Commonwealth of Pennsylvania, 614 A.2d 1106 (Pa. 1992).

[27] 42 Pa.C.S.A. §8934.

[28] Sullivan v. City of Pittsburgh, 561 A.2d 863, 864 (Pa. Commw. Ct. 1989).

[29] Scheetz v. Morning Call, Inc., 747 F.Supp. 1515 (E.D. Pa. 1990).

[30] North Hills News Record v. Town of McCandless, 722 A.2d 1037, 1041 (1999).

were denied. The Commonwealth Court, however, found that report was an essential component and a prerequisite of the Public Welfare Department approval of state hospitals and thus constituted a "decision by an agency fixing the personal or property rights, privileges, immunities, duties or obligations" of the patients and thus was a "public record" under the Act.[31]

Generally, documents constituting an essential component of an agency decision affecting a person or group of persons become public records. A newspaper sought to inspect and copy real estate appraisals of property acquired by the city of Chester. The city had represented that the appraisals were the basis for determining the prices included in the purchase agreement for the residential properties. In ruling for the newspaper, the Commonwealth Court wrote:

> Inasmuch as the appraisals provide the basis for the determination of the prices that the city was willing to pay for these properties, they constitute an essential component of an agency decision facing the personal or property right of a group of persons.32

Compare, however, the result when a *Centre Daily Times* reporter sought to obtain a copy of the county solicitor's memorandum to the Commissioners. Here the newspaper argued that it was entitled to inspect the document because the swing voter on the issue of reclassifying the district attorney's position from part-time to full-time stated that he had relied on the memorandum in switching his vote from his previously stated opinion. The other two Commissioners had been deadlocked on the issue for several years. Although much of

---

[31] Patients of Philadelphia State Hospital v. Commonwealth Dept. of Public Welfare, 417 A.2d 805, 807 (Pa. Commw. Ct. 1980).
[32] City of Chester v. Getak, 572 A.2d 1319, 1320 (Pa. Commw. Ct. 1990).

the third Commissioner's election campaign centered around the reclassification issue, the Commonwealth Court found that the solicitor's memorandum was "not a prerequisite to an agency making a decision and is only 'advice.' Legal opinions are not an 'essential component' of an agency's decision and, hence, not a 'public record.'"[33]

An insurance agent under investigation by the state's Insurance Department sought access to the contents of the administrative agency's file on him. Although the file was being used against him in proceedings and thus broadly affected him, the investigation exception applies, and the Insurance Department did not have to release the file.[34]

Additionally, the commercial motivation of the request for records is irrelevant. The Department of State was required to disclose the names of candidates taking the Certified Public Accountant examination. The requester was a commercial group that conducted C.P.A. exam study courses.[35] Similarly, the Pennsylvania Game Commission had to provide the subscriber list to its publication, *Pennsylvania Game News*, to a commercially motivated requester.[36]

Educational Documents

When parents of kindergarten students, upset with changes in the school-day schedule, sought a list of all the students enrolled in kindergarten, the Commonwealth Court ruled they were entitled to it because it was a record used to determine when the students would be assigned, and thus fixed

---

[33] Nittany Printing & Publishing v. Centre County Board of Commissioners, 627 A.2d 301, 304 (Pa. Commw. Ct. 1993).

[34] Pastore v. Commonwealth Insurance Dept., 558 A.2d 909 (Pa. Commw. Ct. 1989).

[35] Freidman v. Fumo, 309 A.2d 75 (Pa. Commw. Ct. 1973).

[36] Hoffman v. Pennsylvania Game Commission, 455 A.2d 731 (Pa. Commw. Ct. 1983).

"personal property rights, privileges, immunities, duties or obligation of any person or group."[37]

The First Class Township Code provision requires records of civil service examination to be open to the public. Consequently, the grades of police officers taking the sergeant's exam were public records.[38]

Other Highlights of the New Act

The new law permits requests for records to be made in person, by mail, by facsimile or -- if the agency allows -- by any other electronic means. The request should be made to the head of the agency or another person that the agency designates. All requests should specifically identify the records sought and should include name and address where the agency response should be directed.

The requester need not provide a purpose for seeking the record, and the purpose cannot be used as reason for denying the request. If the requested record contains both public information and non-public information, the agency must permit access to the public portion of the record while redacting any information that is not subject to access. The agency must make a effort to respond as promptly as possible, but in any event, Commonwealth agencies must respond within 10 business days and local governmental agencies must respond within business five days.

Appeals from Denial of Access

The new law spells out enhanced procedures that a requester can follow if access to a record is denied. The precise way to proceed depends, in large part, on the nature of the agency making the denial.

The first step in the process is for the requester to file exceptions with the agency head within 15 business days of the

---

[37] Young v. Armstrong School District, 344 A.2d 738, 739 (Pa. Commw. Ct. 1975).
[38] Marvel v. Dalrymple, 393 A.2d 494 (Pa. Commw. Ct. 1978).

mailing date of the agency's response. The exceptions should spell out the grounds upon which the requester believes the record should be considered public. They must also address the basis the agency used to deny or delay the request. Within 30 days of the requester's mailing of the exceptions, the agency head or designee must make a final determination and notify the requester. The agency is permitted to hold a hearing on the matter before making that determination.

The second form of protesting the agency's denial is by judicial appeal. If a requester is filing an appeal to a Commonwealth agency's denial of access, he or she must first file exceptions. If the request was made to a non-Commonwealth agency, the requester can file exceptions or proceed directly to judicial appeal. Commonwealth agency appeals must be made to the Commonwealth Court within 30 days of the final determination. Non-commonwealth agency appeals must be made to the Court of Common Pleas within 30 days of the denial or final determination. The new act provides an option for making the appeal to a district justice, but the Pennsylvania Supreme Court suspended that provision as the law took effect "partially because district justices do not issue written decisions routinely."[39] The Supreme Court is expected to make a final decision on the appropriateness of appealing to the minor judiciary after reviewing recommendations of its rules committee.

Pennsylvania Sunshine Act

The Pennsylvania Sunshine Act, which replaced the former Open Meetings Law in 1987, is based upon the principle that the democratic process requires openness. Consequently, the legislature recognized a right of the public to be present at the "deliberation, policy formulation and decision making of agencies."[40]

---

[39] PNPA Report, Issue No. 1,066, April 1, 2003, p. 1.
[40] 65 Pa.C.S.A. § 702.

Agencies include the governmental body and Committees that "take official action or render advice on matters of agency business."[41] The Statute specifically includes school boards, state-owned, state-aided and state-related university boards and councils of trustees. Agency business is defined as the "framing, preparation, making or enactment of laws, policy or regulations, the creation of liability by contract or otherwise or adjudication of rights, duties and responsibilities, but not including administrative action."[42]

The 1987 Sunshine Act made a significant departure from the earlier statute. Under the previous Open Meeting Law, governing bodies had to hold an open meeting *only* to vote or make policy. The discussions leading up to the vote could be held in closed work sessions and often were. Under the Sunshine Law, "deliberation," defined as "the discussion of agency business held for the purposes of making a decision" must be conducted at a public meeting.[43] In all of the process, however, an element of trust in government officials is required; hence, officials must want to guard the law vigorously in order for it to work. To be sure, Pennsylvania's courts, through interpretation, have carved out enough escape hatches so that significant work could be carried out in cloture.

Executive Sessions

The statute also recognizes times when agency business should, for specific reasons, be conducted privately. Consequently, the Sunshine Act provides for "executive sessions"[44] for the following reasons:

(1) discussion of employment terms or disciplinary action of a current, former, or prospective public officer or employee.

---

[41] 65 Pa. C.S.A. § 703.
[42] Id.
[43] Id.
[44] 65 Pa. C.S.A. § 708.

(2) collective bargaining strategy or negotiation sessions.

(3) consideration of the purchase or lease of real property.

(4) consultation with legal and other professional counsel about litigation or "issues on which identifiable complaints are expected to be filed."

(5) discussion of business which, if made public, would violate a privilege or disclose a confidentiality protected by law.

(6) discussion of academic admission or students by state-owned, state-aided or state-related boards or councils of trustees.

Cases from Commonwealth Court help clarify the reasons for executive session. Very few published opinions on Sunshine Act cases have been handed down in the last decade, but one of the more important ones helped to ameliorate the problem of governmental bodies declaring an executive session for a generic reason, e.g., "We're going into executive session to discuss personnel." When the Reading City Council was called to task for such transgressions, the Commonwealth Court observed that the General Assembly's intent in requiring agencies to give a reason for going into executive session was to provide the public the ability "to determine from the reason given whether they are being properly excluded from the session."[45] To this end, the Court said, "...the reasons stated by the public agency must be specific, indicating a real, discrete matter that is best addressed in private."[46]

The timing of executive sessions varies from agency to agency. They are sometimes held before the regular meeting begins, during a break, at the end or at a future time. Agency members, however, must take care not to engage privately in

---

[45] Reading Eagle Co. v. Council of City of Reading, 627 A.2d 305 (Pa. Commw. Ct. 1993).

[46] Id. at 307.

what may be characterized as "deliberations" under the Act. The Commonwealth Court, for example, found that "deliberations" did occur when three members of a township board of supervisors discussed a zoning ordinance amendment on the afternoon of a regularly scheduled meeting. The private conference was an effort to inform a recent appointee to the board about the issue. The Court concluded: "Because there was discussion of the agency business at the conference, obviously toward the purpose of ultimately making a decision at some time, we conclude that 'deliberations,' as defined under Section 3 of the Act, occurred between the group members at the afternoon conference."[47]

Executive sessions present the most troublesome part of the act for the news media and the public. Often times the issues in which they are most interested are discussed in these sessions. It is useful to note that while the establishment of policy must be done at a public meeting, the execution of that policy may be carried out privately as part of the "administrative action" provision of the law. Accordingly, when Johnstown's mayor laid off police officers (without any public decision) because the city council had not passed a budget by the end of the year, no violation of the Sunshine Act occurred. The mayor was carrying out an administrative act in light of the budget defeat at an earlier *public* city council meeting.[48]

The Commonwealth Court in 2000 clarified the issue of whether an informational meeting must be open to the public. Informational meetings designed to bring members of the board "up-to-date" or provide a status report on a particular project are not required to be open as long as no action is taken.[49]

---

[47] Ackerman v. Upper Mt. Bethel Township, 567 A.2d 1116, 1119 (Pa. Commw. Ct. 1989).

[48] Fraternal Order of Police, Flood City Lodge No. 86 v. City of Johnstown, 594 A.2d 838 (Pa. Commw. Ct. 1990).

[49] Belitskus v. Hamlin Township, 764 A.2d 669, 672 (Pa. Commw. Ct. 2000)

Conduct of Meetings

The legislature has codified the right of the public to have a reasonable opportunity to be heard at regular and special meetings of boards, councils and authorities of political subdivisions in the state.[50] The comment period, which typically takes place at the beginning of meetings, may be deferred if sufficient time is not available for the public to be heard at that time.

The Act provides for recording devices at meetings, but is silent with respect to video recording devices.[51] Commonwealth Court helped to clarify the provision in 1994, holding that it is improper under the Sunshine Act to prohibit videotaping of agency meetings.[52] Agencies, however, are permitted to adopt rules respecting the maintenance of order at meetings, provided that the intent of the Act is not violated,[53] and the Court found that "an agency may restrain [videotaping] by reasonable rules designed to maintain order."[54]

Sanctions

Anyone who wishes to challenge an agency must do so within 30 days of an open meeting or discovery of the illegal action taken at that meeting or within one year of a closed meeting. If the court finds a violation did occur, it may nullify any or all official action taken at the meeting.[55] Agency members who intentionally participated in the illegal meeting may be convicted of a summary offense.

---

[50] 65 Pa.C.S.A. § 710.1.
[51] 65 Pa.C.S.A. § 711.
[52] Hain v. Board of School Directors of Reading School District, 641 A.2d 661 (Pa. Commw. Ct. 1994).
[53] 65 Pa.C.S.A § 710.
[54] Hain, 641 A.2d at 664, n.2.
[55] 65 Pa. C.S.A. § 713.

www.ingramcontent.com/pod-product-compliance
Lightning Source LLC
Chambersburg PA
CBHW060607210326
41519CB00014B/3589